A practical approach to what you need to know before becoming an ***Entrepreneur!***

The Game Plan for Entrepreneurs

Discovering Your Own Passion and Vision!

by
Creed W. Pannell, Jr.

W0005506

Published by CWPJ Publishers,
a subsidiary of Positive Publications, Inc.
4405 Mall Blvd., Suite 520, Union City, GA 30291

The Game Plan for Entrepreneurs
by Creed W. Pannell, Jr.

Published by CWPJ Publishers,
a subsidiary of Positive Publications, Inc.
4405 Mall Blvd., Suite 520, Union City, GA 30291

This book or parts thereof may not be reproduced in any form, stored in a retrieval system, or transmitted in any form by any means—electronic, mechanical, photocopy, recording, or otherwise—without prior written permission of the publisher, except as provided by United States copyright law.

Copyright ©2009 by Creed W. Pannell, Jr.
ALL RIGHTS RESERVED

How to Order:
Additional copies of this book can be purchased through CWPJ Publishers:

- Online: www.thegameplanbook.com
- Phone: 770.969.7711 Fax: 770.969.7811
- Email: CWPJPublishers@bellsouth.net

Library of Congress Catalog:
    Bibliographical References included.

Arranged and compiled by G. Lynne Alston-Leonard
Designed by Dana R. Taylor

ISBN 0-615-28335-7
ISBN 978-0-615-28335-7
Printed in the United States of America

Table of Contents

Acknowledgements	xi
Preface	xv

Chapter One:
Life's Experiences
1

Chapter Two:
Essentials for the Game
13

Faith	14
The Right Mate	15
Fatherhood and Family	17

Chapter Three:
Using Your Imagination
23

Chapter Four:
Recognizing Your God Given Talents
27

Chapter Five:
Personal Survival Skills
31

A Common Sense Approach to Staying Healthy	32
Music	34
Quiet Time	37
Learn to Laugh	39
Hobbies – Releasing Energy	40
Saying "No" to Drugs or Alcoholism	41

Chapter Six:
It's Your Move!
43

Is Entrepreneurship Right for You?	45
What Resources Do I Need?	47
Preparing To Enter the Game Of Entrepreneurship!	50
Personal Considerations	51
Strategic Business Considerations	52
Business Advisors	54
Business Development and Planning	55
Operations and Start-Up	57
Your Business Mortality	60
The Future of Entrepreneurship	61
What is Social Entrepreneurship?	64

Chapter Seven:
Exploring And Building Strategic Options
67

Travel	68
Networking	69
Playing the Political Game	72

Chapter Eight:
Taking Stock Of YOu
75

How Others View You	76
Honing Your Skills	77
Dealing With Rejection	78
Planning Your Exit	80

Chapter Nine:
The Wisdom Of Success!
83

Service is the Price You Pay … 84
Importance of Volunteerism … 85

Chapter Ten:
Keeping Life Simple…
89

Bibliography … 92
Index … 95

Appendices
100

Appendix 1:
Do You Really Want To Join the Entrepreneur Club? … 101

Appendix 2:
Business and Industry Resources For Entrepreneurs … 102

Appendix 3:
Business and Marketing Planning Resources and Tools for Entrepreneurs … 107

Appendix 4:
Networking Organizations and Associations for Entrepreneurs … 116

Appendix 5:
Resources on Social Entrepreneurship … 118

Appendix 6:
Government and Certification Resources … 120

About the Author … 123

Dedication

This book is dedicated to my wife, Rochelle Render Pannell. She has demonstrated the true spirit of partnership through her love, devotion, and understanding as my wife, and in the many roles she has managed throughout our entrepreneurship relationship. Because of you, we have reaped the benefits of owning our own businesses. Because of you, we have seen the results of our efforts to create opportunities for other entrepreneurs through the products we have created.

It has been your dedication of time, and commitment to our family that helped make our dreams—a reality. No truer words were ever written than, "No man is an island, entire of itself." (Wikisource contributors 2008) All of the events, publications, and products created through the years are dedicated to you—my mate, my love, and my partner.

Thank you.

Acknowledgements

From the day we met, courted, and married, I have known that Rochelle Render Pannell was the "right mate" for me. Much of the wisdom and understanding of what it takes to be a successful entrepreneur would not have been possible without the support and dedication of my wife.

We have been co-partners in every aspect of our lives together—raising a family, spiritual growth and development, the conception and development of successful business ventures. We have traveled the world together. And, together—with discipline, dedication, and hard work—we have persevered in pursuing our dreams successfully.

Again, thank you Rochelle! You have done it all—helping us to achieve our many milestones together.

To my mother and father—I give you thanks for your structure of family values. It has helped to strengthen me and guide me in living life to its fullest. I thank you for providing me with a beautiful life in a small town—full of the strong values exemplified by all those I encountered while growing up in that small community of Virginia.

Because of you, I've learned the importance my environment played during my formative years—the family, extended family, and caring adults who reminded me of the importance of good manners, etiquette, community involvement, a spiritual church foundation, and the principles of dedicated hard work. This solid foundation stuck with me; and paved the way for my success as a man, husband, father, grandfather, and entrepreneur. More importantly, it instilled in me the desire and passion for making our communities, our nation, and the world a better place.

To my kids—thank you for your understanding, encouragement, and support in helping to make our family's business ventures successful. I pray that this book will serve as a legacy for you to pass on to your children…it reflects an accumulation of a wealth of knowledge passed on to me from my parents, experienced and shared by me, and now passed on to you. May this legacy be used to benefit generations that will follow.

Thank you to all of my other business associates, too numerous to mention, for all of your help along the way. I look forward to the many challenges and new business relationships that will come as a result of our world travels, and continued development of new business ventures.

To the many readers who will view this book—thank you for allowing me to share my experiences, and what fifty plus years as an entrepreneur has taught me. As I pass on **my** Game Plan for Entrepreneurs, I urge you to always learn from each and every venture you endeavor. There are no failures, only windows of opportunity for new visions—new dreams—that can take you to another level.

I hope this book will enable you to find and focus on your vision and passions for your life, your community, and the world in which we live. I urge you to call upon, trust, and depend on your spirit guide; and to be led by your vision and passion for better relationships with your family, humankind, and community as you seek to establish and/or reinvent your business ventures.

I hope that you will gain understanding and an appreciation of the impact and influence that family, spiritual growth, development, and personal relationships can have on your own personal and business growth. Never take them lightly, or for granted. They are keys to your success as an individual, and a businessperson.

If you are contemplating entrepreneurship for the first time, or seeking answers rebuilding or growing an existing business, the time is now—make a commitment to becoming all that you can be as an entrepreneur. Find the passion and gain your confidence—you must believe in your own ideas and visions for the future. Know that it is yours for the taking—if you but ask, and prepare yourself with a positive foundation. When you honor God's request to be "your brother's keeper," so shall you reap. A positive approach to life through all that you do, will result in a positive outcome for all that you seek.

To Lynne Alston-Leonard—thank you for your hard work and dedication in helping to complete this book. I could not have done it without you. Through the years, and many projects and work together, we have come to know that our meeting was truly in Divine order.

And last, but always first, I thank God for all that you have done for me—and will do for me.

I am your witness… what follows is my testimony!

Preface

The main purpose of this book is to inspire you and offer a more practical approach for you to include in your deliberations and preparations for your journey or career as an entrepreneur—a journey that can be very rewarding, yet challenging. Entrepreneurship offers the opportunity for you to update your resume in life as you build your business, stirred by the constant desire to create and seek new ideas for growth and change. Most importantly, the journey provides an opportunity to create and leave a legacy for generations to carry on.

To the next generation of entrepreneurs yet to become a part of this club, I hope this book will help to answer many of your questions, and serve as a "checklist" that will help you to lay a foundation to "step out on faith" and find the entrepreneur within.

To those of you who have already begun your journey into entrepreneurship, this book seeks to help you attain a greater understanding of your own passion, vision, and purpose as an entrepreneur through this practical approach to entrepreneurship, and the insights presented which are the result of more than fifty years experience as a successful entrepreneur. May you find some benefit from the wisdom shared as you contemplate your development as a successful entrepreneur, or the growth and development of your business venture in today's global economy.

May God bless you and keep you throughout your journey!

Chapter 1

Life Experiences

> "*The young do not know enough to be prudent, and therefore they attempt the impossible — and achieve it, generation after generation.*"
>
> – Pearl S. Buck (Buck 1995-2009)

I have been an entrepreneur most of my life. For more than 30 years, I have gone about "the business" of creating and establishing successful business ventures, including: CEO and founder of Positive Publications, Inc. (PPI), a publishing group for the Atlanta Business Journal Magazine, the Atlanta NewsLeader newspaper, the Weddings For Us Bridal Magazine, and Atlanta Metro monthly tabloid; Chairman and Executive Producer of the Annual Gospel Choice Awards (AGCA), the Georgia Minority Business Awards (GMBA), Youth Gospel Choice Awards (YGCA), Weddings For Us (WFU) Bridal Expo; a managing partner in ventures such as It's YourChoice Natural Gas, and The Gospel Express; and my initial ventures as a national sales/marketing consultant and manufacturer's representative for other businesses.

Over the years, I have often been asked what my secret to success has been. It has been suggested several times that I write a book that would share my story, and give insight into my success.

First off, if one believes that there is power in your name—then I must say that my life as a successful entrepreneur as been led by my own *creed:*

To be successful as a businessman, I must strive everyday to be successful in all that I do—as a businessman, a husband, a father, a grandfather, a great-grandfather, a friend, a mentor, and a faithful servant to God.

"He has achieved success who has lived well, laughed often and loved much; who has gained the respect of intelligent men and the love of little children; who has filled his niche and accomplished his task; who has left the world better than he found it, whether by an improved poppy, a perfect poem, or a rescued soul; who has never lacked appreciation of earth's beauty or failed to express it;

who has always looked for the best in others and given them the best he had; whose life was an inspiration; whose memory a benediction." (Stanley 1905)

Because many of you may not have had the benefit of growing up with parents or other relatives that had the luxury of starting their own businesses, you may not recognize your own aptitude for entrepreneurship. You may not feel you have the confidence to dream about non-traditional opportunities for your future.

What follows is my story, my testimony to all that God has given me.

I was born and raised in Staunton, Virginia, to parents that instilled the value of education, discipline, character, self-worth, and responsibility in their children. Staunton was a small community, where everyone knew everyone else. Thus began my lessons in life.

My grandfather was a minister for 49 years in the community. He was an entrepreneur, starting a church that grew to become a pillar in the community. He had a vision and developed the leadership skills to build a church that became central to stability and health of the community.

The question of attending church was not an option. Although the Ministry was not my calling, through the church I garnered faith to believe in myself, the importance of belonging to an organization, the opportunity to witness many who helped to lay the foundation for building character among the young, and the importance of honoring God through helping others.

I grew up experiencing the struggles and successes of small business owners—my relatives were successful business owners of the Pannells Inn (a small motel that catered to African-Americans who could not yet stay in traditional hotels in the city), and a local barbershop. Like most small towns in the early to mid-1900s, you had to create your own businesses in order to have access to the goods and services you wanted or needed. My family and community consisted of several generations of educated people who had become veterinarians, doctors, ministers, pharmacists, and entrepreneurs in their own right. In fact, my maternal grandfather used his brick masonry skills to build many of the homes and businesses in the area.

By the time, I was six or seven years old, I had already begun to recognize and understand something called "racism." I was already being taught that "we" had to do things different and better than *others did* in order to get ahead. And, that hard work, honesty, integrity, and belief in oneself are vital to becoming a man.

My father, a World War II veteran, had gone to war and returned a different man. Disillusioned, he was no longer able to become the man he once wanted to become. The dreams he had for his family would have to be attained in different ways.

The doors that remained closed to him upon his return, forced him to teach us to be independent and aware of our surroundings. Raising a family with seven children was difficult, but we made it—and were somehow very happy in spite of the absence and influence of television. As a family, we learned how to communicate with others around the dining room table.

My father taught me that no matter what your job or station in life, it was important to be committed to providing for your family—doing whatever it took—with pride, integrity, and honesty. My father showed me the value of being kind, and respected by all; and the necessity and importance of always working hard to attain the things or relationships you value in life. He showed me that hard work never hurts anyone. He insisted that his children keep at least a B+ average in school; and that we had to keep a part-time job, and perform household chores as long as we lived in his house. Most important, he taught me that respect from others must be earned.

My mother worked as a librarian's aide in a college library, cleaned offices, and helped out with private parties for the "well-to-do." She taught all of her children how to cook, clean house, take care of ourselves, and supported each of us in our extracurricular activities—from sports, science and math competitions, to band and choir competitions. In other words, she made sure we kept busy all of the time.

My mother was great at managing money. She taught us "how money works," the value and importance of saving, and the willingness to take risks through investing your money.

Little did I know; I was already on the road to developing some of the qualities essential to becoming a successful businessperson. I would venture to say that some of the most successful entrepreneurs demonstrated some of the same potential, early in life.

My brother used to deliver papers for the Washington Post, and I would often go with him to help him out along his route. I even adapted to getting up at 4:00 AM every morning (something most nine year old boys don't like to do), to help him out.

A few years later, after talking to a newspaper boy that delivered the local newspaper to my neighborhood, I decided I wanted to try it out. I was twelve years old when I took a job as the first African-American "paper boy" for the Staunton NewsLeader, the City's number-one paper.

Suddenly, a whole "new world" opened up for me. My paper route took me to parts of town I had never seen, and through neighborhoods filled with lifestyles I had yet to experience. I delivered papers and established relationships with the mayor, judges, teachers, college presidents, and other business leaders in the community. I even had the publisher of my newspaper as a client.

My athletic abilities and competitiveness also played a part in my development as a "young entrepreneur." On many days, along my route, I stopped to play a little "pick up" ball with the white kids who thought they could beat me because our high school teams had competed. I soon became invited to join in whenever I was in the neighborhood delivering papers. I was smart enough to know that I was invited to play because I was black and a better athlete, and could possibly help their game. Little did they know; I was a willing participant because it gave me an opportunity to further develop relationships and awareness of people from mixed incomes and different ethnic, cultural, and religious backgrounds. In turn, they grew comfortable enough to ask and try to understand why we went to different schools, and why the school system was segregated.

My earlier lessons in character building, kindness, dedication, and commitment to doing a job well became my weapon for overcoming the obstacles of racism....sure it existed...but I soon learned that providing good customer service and being professional would take me one step closer to bigger opportunities.

You would be surprised at how much respect (or perhaps a bit of curiosity) is raised by being a polite and respectful "little black boy," who delivered the paper on time—through rain, sleet, or snow, threw it in the right place, and was courteous and accurate when it came to weekly visits to collect fees for their paper subscriptions—most likely, atypical of their expectations.

I soon learned that I enjoyed making money, and that I made even more by providing better customer service. I also learned that to make money, I had to be good at collecting money….so I studied and learned when it was the best time to collect for weekly subscription fees…It was too costly if I had to come back and forth.

As the success on my newspaper job grew, my father taught me never to spend all my money on foolish things and girls (even though I would be called cheap by their standards), and that I must always remember to thank God for the many blessings I received by giving to my church. And since my mother had already shown me the value of saving, it was not long before I had a nice little savings account through the newspaper savings plan.

I had also learned that it was important to share whatever success I had, no matter how small or large, with others. And so, I shared the "wealth" with my friends. I started hiring other kids to help me on my paper route. Initially, I hired two boys to deliver the papers, while I managed the collection of the monies. As word spread about our customer service, our customers began to refer new customers. Over the next five years, my route would grow from 50 to 275 customers, with a crew of two kids helping me.

I had soon learned enough to successfully build a business and manage my own time. So much so, that the father of one of the Jewish young men I had befriended along my route, soon took notice and offered me another part-time job while I was still in high school. I worked 10 to 15 hours per week in one of the City's finest jewelry stores.

There, I became exposed to a different type of business, and interacted with another type of customer. In addition to helping to keep the store clean, and the jewelry cases sparkling, the owner trusted me enough to teach me the skill of "etching" or engraving a name or initials for a customer on fine jewelry, or glass. I had gotten my first glimpse of how Jewish people built and ran businesses.

It was here that I also began to learn how they studied their surroundings for future decisions. For example, the son of the owner taught me the "lay of the land" as it related to higher academic institutions in Virginia. He explained, for example, that the University of Virginia was known for graduating lawyers who went on to pursue careers within the Washington, DC legal system; William and Mary College graduates pursued careers in the CIA and FBI; graduates of the military schools such as VMI or VPI went on to work at the Pentagon; and that women's colleges in Virginia primarily prepared their graduates for the role as "wife" for these strong, political, legal, and military men who have graduated from the Virginia institutions of higher learning.

It is important to note, that I did all of this—and then some—while maintaining better than a B+ average in high school—as required in my household—and also continued to excel in competitive sports, other extracurricular activities.

I had learned how to build a business, and juggle priorities between schoolwork, church, athletics, household chores, a dishwashing job in a local college-dining hall, my part-time job at the jewelry store, and my paper route. Before graduating, I held a summer internship position as a ward assistant at the one of our city's local mental health institutions. Though it was often scary, I remember feeling extremely rewarded and satisfied having performed a job where I could assist those that were not able to help themselves.

By the time I graduated from high school, I already had a sense of "empowerment," and possibility…a whole new world ahead of me as an entrepreneur.

When I left Staunton, Virginia, I moved to Washington, DC to attend Howard University. There I met students from all over the world, and worked part-time at the U.S. Post Office to help meet expenses—as many students did at that time.

My first job after college was as a Food Director for several dining establishments on the campuses of Chaney State University and Lincoln University. I later became a division sales manager for the Pillsbury Company. I went on to complete a journalism program, after receiving a scholarship to the Charles Price School of Journalism in Philadelphia.

I later moved to Jacksonville, Florida to become a Regional Manager for Helen Curtis Industries, responsible for sales in their northeast and southern markets. As usual, I excelled in my job—winning all of their national sales and marketing awards.

At this point in my life, I realized that I was not happy in "Corporate America." I believed I had a calling for something else, as was armed with enough experience to head out on my own. I discovered that I had a passion to help the smaller minority-owned health and beauty aids companies become successful. It was then that I extended my experience to help launch Care Free Curl and Leisure Curl Products companies to develop national strategies for growth.

I would ultimately lend my services to more than 20 companies, helping them become major players in the health, beauty, and cosmetic industries. Because of my experience with African-American health, and beauty products, I was hired to serve as a consultant to major retailers on the design of plan-o-grams for their black haircare sections.

I was happy, and well on my way to becoming a successful entrepreneur.

Years later, I would honor the memory of my experience as just a "paper boy" at the Staunton NewsLeader—the place where I first discovered the entrepreneur in me, developed my early business skills, and gained a greater appreciation for the values my parents and ancestors had given me. I would ultimately name my second media venture, the Atlanta NewsLeader.

I would be remiss; if I did not point out that, I recognize and have often faced obstacles as an African-American male trying to venture into the business world. My background and family have taught me how important it is to not let any prejudices or biases hinder me in whatever I endeavor. Regardless of whether you are black or white, Asian or Hispanic, male or female, it is incumbent upon you to know and believe that you too can achieve all that you dream and desire according to God's plan.

Family life is full of major and minor crises — the ups and downs of health, success, and failure in career, marriage, and divorce — and all kinds of characters. It is tied to places and events and histories. With all of these felt details, life etches itself into memory and personality. It's difficult to imagine anything more nourishing to the soul.

Thomas Moore (Moore n.d.)

Chapter 2

Essentials for the Game

"A man without ambition is dead. A man with ambition but no love is dead. A man with ambition and love for his blessings here on earth is ever so alive."

Bailey, Pearl Entertainer (1918-1990)

I thank God everyday for His love, and then for the gift of the love of my wife, and that of my family. For they are all the reasons for my success! They are my lifeline to infinite possibilities.

Faith

When your great-grandfather is a Baptist minister, you spend a great bit of time in church. You grow up with a foundation deeply rooted in faith, and the belief of the presence of God in your life.

Through the church, and the on-going testing of my own faith in God, I have grown to understand that God will—indeed—place before you all that you need, if you ask. Having been raised to participate in church, and to seek and trust God for His spiritual guidance and support no matter what, I have leaned on Him throughout my life as an entrepreneur.

I remember when I began a business venture as "an independent manufacturer's representative" for several successful companies. And like the newspaper route I had many years before, I built a successful business for the companies by establishing a team of independent sales representatives who relied upon me for their livelihoods.

With a thriving business, my number one company soon advised me that they were going to give 80% of the business I built for them to another contracted group. I was, essentially, left to start all over again....only this time, I had several others who relied upon the business we built for these companies to take care of their families as well.

I felt a sense of responsibility to them...and knew I had to do something. And, so—I prayed! I took it to God, and asked Him, "What do I do next?"

The first thing He did was to help provide a way for me to find employment for my team that had to be disbanded.

The second thing He did was to lead me to another church...a church that would help me grow stronger spiritually...a church where greater opportunities would be presented, and a ministry that would speak to my inner spirit.

From a business perspective, He helped me see that it was time to re-invent myself. I would never again allow any one client or company to control more than 30% of the income of my business ventures.

Although I was raised a Christian, my journey has taken me into many churches, among many people, of all races, and all religions. The most important message for me to convey is that no one can or will achieve his or her potential without belief and faith in God—no matter what you call Him or Her. You must believe and have faith in a power greater than you have.

The Right Mate

To believe in the power and love of God, is to be open to His gifts of love and community, offered to us for the constant nurturing of our spirit and soul—to keep us whole. If we were to truly embrace the African concept of "it takes a village," we would understand that it teaches us that there is nothing in life we can do alone. The Dagara people of West Africa remind us to "look at our understanding of intimacy as primarily a practice ordered by spirit, or authorized by spirit; and executed by someone who recognizes that she (he) cannot, by herself (himself), make happen what she (he) has been invited toward." (Some 1997)

The community and love that will surround you, embrace you, and encourage you during the peaks and valleys of entrepreneurship begins and ends with you. It acknowledges the spirit within that guides you to choose a partner and a relationship that is spirit-driven. If all of us were to consider some of the African traditions of our ancestors, we might better understand and value the role of "our mate" or life partner. "Marriage is two soles coming into one soul—still distinct but forming one entity. It is a way of bringing two people's gifts together in order to strengthen them and make them even better. It acknowledges that two people are embarking on something that is bigger than them and bigger than the tribe." (Some 1997)

As an entreprenuer, it is imperative that your mate understand what it means for *you* to be an entreprenuer—that she/he be secure in herself/himself, and is fully aware of the time and financial commitments it takes to be a successful entreprenuer. Moreover, it is important that your mate share in your mission, ideals, and vision; and be willing to participate in helping you to meet your goals and objectives. As a couple, you must have open discussions regarding your plans—both personal and business. You should identify opportunities for both of you to share in the growth and devleopment of your venture. For example, if your mate's strength is in finance or accounting, while yours is sales and marketing, be open to receiving and utilizing the expertise of your mate.

At the same time, it is equally important that you share in your mates personal and career aspirations. If your mate has a vision for other opportunities, be a willing partner...take time to listen to her/his dreams and seek opportunities that are mutually beneficial to both of you. Whatever you do, never take the posture that your mate's visions and goals must be put off until you have successfully achieved yours.

In my case, my wife always had visions of being a wedding consultant. While she supported my business ventures, I utilized my business expertise to help her successfully build the Weddings For Us franchise—a magazine, bridal show, private event facility, and more.

Building trust between you and your mate is criticial. Both of you must trust each other not to "sabotage" the other's dream for the sake of achieving one's own. This important trust factor is key to accepting constructive criticism or comments relative to ideas or concepts that may disagree or negate your initial thinking. This is important, as your mate is the one who will be most honest in helping to evaluate any plans or new ideas.

Over the years, I have seen too many people achieve success in business ventures, or their chosen professions—yet they are still unhappy, unfulfilled. In my lifetime, I have learned that to be blessed with love of my wife, keeps me whole. It keeps me driven and motivated in business for all the right reasons. It keeps me balanced. It gives me someone to share my successes with.

Fatherhood and Family

To be a father is to know and understand that your children are another gift from God. You have been entrusted with the responsibility for their care and nurturing. They are God's seed for the future of our world.

To become truly successful as both a father and an entrepreneur, you must first realize that your desire for success as an entrepreneur is *your dream*, your passion for demonstrating your God given talents whenever and however you choose. It is the realization of the hopes and dreams instilled in you, nurtured and inspired by your father, your mother, your family, your ancestors—your village. It is not yet, the dream of your child.

To achieve success as father, while pursuing your dreams as an entrepreneur, is to remember that you have been entrusted with nurturing the character, aspirations, and hopes of a child who has yet to learn how to dream. There is no other responsibility given to us greater than the role of parent.

You and your spouse become the primary role models for your children. The only way to teach a child to be faithful, respectful, confident, assured, successful, tolerant, and honest is to demonstrate it as a parent. When becoming a successful businessperson takes priority over your role as a parent, then you will have failed in honoring God and the village that guided and inspired you.

The needs of your children must always remain in view of your personal, emotional, and business radar screen. If you find this difficult, then accept and rely on your mate to keep you apprised of critical times in their lives that are important for you to participate. They deserve quality time from you, just as your work requires quality time.

There were often times that my business schedule seemed that it might interfere with my obligations and commitments to my children. But, I was determined to sacrifice what I had to do—to be the best father I could, in spite of my business goals

I'm here to tell you—there are no words to express the tremendous satisfaction I felt after seeing my children's faces lit up when they saw me sitting in the bleachers or the bandstands watching them cheering on their school team, or playing in the band during events they thought I would miss. There is no amount of profit, nor business sacrifice that can outweigh the joy of knowing you were there for your children.

As your children grow up, find ways that you can include them in your business venture...if for no other reason than to show them why you, as their parent, have been so busy.

Your children will benefit more than you realize when you expose them to what you do. As early as three years of age, start talking to them about what you do. When they are ready:

- Take them with you to your place of business.
- Introduce them to some of the smaller chores or tasks of your business.
- Teach them how their time is valuable to their own growth and knowledge.
- Teach them how to build relationships.
- Introduce them to the rewards of owning your own business.
- Talk to them about Profit and Loss, and accountability.
- Introduce them to success stories of the young and successful people in careers within their culture.
- Take them to events where you are presented an award for your business efforts or contributions to the community and humankind. Help them feel a sense of pride for you as parent, and for himself or herself as the son or daughter of a "winner."

Now that my children are adults, they lead their own lives, but have continued to actively, and joyfully participate in various aspects of our businesses. You will find them with me...backstage helping with the Gospel Award shows, Weddings For Us Bridal Expos; at the registration desk for our annual GMBA dinner, reviewing and editing scripts or articles; or making sales presentations for our natural gas venture, etc.

Always remember, your children are your future. They will become who and what you help them grow into!

Try not to become a man of success but rather try to become a man of value.
               Albert Einstein (Einstein n.d.)

Chapter 3

Using Your Imagination

The world is but a canvas to the imagination.
　　　　　　　Henry David Thoreau (Thoreau n.d.)

One of the jobs my father held when I was growing up was that of a janitor in the barracks on the campus of a local military school in Staunton. He was well liked. He often received tokens of appreciation from faculty and administrators he served.

Many of the cadets would give him the comic books that were being discarded by their peers. And of course, my father would bring them home to me.

I soon discovered that I had an incredible appetite for the "old classic" comic books—Archie & Friends, Richie Rich, Batman & Robin, Superman, the Hulk, Spiderman, etc. I was fascinated by the illustrations, and taken by the visions of the creators of the comic book heroes.

I read everything from comic books, to classic novels, westerns, comedy, etc. At a young age, it was a way for me to explore the world—to look outside my community and envision a world of possibilities.

By now you're asking, "How did reading comic books and other novels have an impact on me as an entrepreneur?"

The answer is very simple:

- *The comic book characters from 50 years ago, gave me an opportunity to visit other cultures, and the visionaries of their worlds—I was inspired to travel beyond the boundaries of worlds beyond my own small town.*
- *Reading comic books and novels of interest kept my attention, kept me out of trouble, and helped me improve my reading and speed reading abilities.*
- *Collecting and trading comic books enhanced my bartering skills.*
- *Reading comic books helped to stimulate my own imagination*

> *and quite possibly, another spiritual force leading me to become a media publisher.*

Over the years, readers of comic books became collectors of comic books—a very valuable hobby. At some point in time, I imagine that it was a passionate collector who first developed his love for trading and swapping comic books into a business venture that opened doors to a world of possibilities yet to be discovered.

My only regret is that I did not keep my comic books—as collector items they would be worth millions. *But then, I realized that was not a part of God's plan for me.*

I know that reading comic books have been a source for stimulating my imagination and creativity. You must find yours. Is it sci-fi movies, looking up at the stars, mountain visits, staring out over the ocean or across the lake, daydreaming, or something else? Only you can answer that question for yourself.

Chapter 4

Recognizing Your God Given Talents

"Find out how much God has given you and from it, take what you need; the remainder is needed by others."

-Saint Augustine
(Augustine, Brainy Quotes
-St. Augustine Quote n.d.)

I believe that most people have potential that far exceeds their level of contribution or participation in most business, civic, or social settings. For many, limitations have been unconsciously set, given one's own perspective, professional, or personal definition of what it takes to make it—to be successful in whatever endeavors once chooses to pursue, or to become the "hero," role model, or leader you have in mind.

Often times, we have failed to thoroughly examine our own God given talents that may help us better define who we are, or what we can do.

For example, think back to your childhood or youth—what skills, hobbies, or interests did you have that would lend themselves to an entrepreneurial venture? Did you enjoy singing, writing, music, handiwork, assembling miniature cars or airplanes, cooking, crafts, sewing, water sports, public speaking, acting, teaching, or collecting things?

If so, then you have probably demonstrated some of the key characteristics or traits required of a successful entrepreneur:

Selling abilities
Did you ever set up a lemonade stand or sell dinners to make extra money?

Leadership
Did you constantly initiate activities (constructive or not) as a young person? Did you get others to go along with your ideas or plans?

Creativity
Were you constantly developing opportunities that allowed you to express your creative thinking?

Speaking abilities
Were you confident in presenting your ideas or thoughts before your class, peers, or others?

Organization
Did you have to plan a menu, determine the supplies or equipment you would need, or identify the type of help you would need to execute your idea?

If any of these traits or experiences are reflective of you or the dreams you had as a youth, then entrepreneurship might be a viable option for you. I encourage you, as Marian Wright Edelman so aptly stated in her commencement address to the graduating class of Tarbut V'Torah in Irvine, California, to "...listen to the sound of the genuine in yourself. ' Small,' Einstein said, 'is the number of them who see with their own eyes and feel with their own heart.' Try to be one of them. There is something in every one of you that waits and listens for the sound of the genuine in ourselves. And it is the only true guide we will ever have, if you cannot hear it in yourself, you will spend all of your life on the end of strings that somebody else pulls. Today there are just so many noises and so many competing pulls on us. I hope that you'll find ways and times and spaces to be silent to listen to yourselves..." (Edelman 2004)

I realized early in life that I had been given the gift of salesmanship, leadership, and speaking. Over time, I have been able to turn these gifts and my passion for economic development within the African American communities into successful ventures as a consultant for African American-owned business enterprises, and as a champion for opening doors for little known gospel artists, or up and coming minority-owned ventures. I have taken my obligation to God, and my responsibility as a leader to help nurture and promote the gifts and talents of others—young and old.

Do you recognize the gifts and talents God has given you? If you're not sure, ask your friends, family, or business associates what they would identify as your gifts and talents. It may also be helpful if you start by assessing your strengths and weaknesses.

Once you've identified your own gifts and talents, where will they take you. How will you use all that God has given you?

Chapter 5

Personal Survival Skills

"If the good life means plenty of fast food to eat and plenty of machines to do our work for us and entertain us so we don't have to get out of our chairs, well, the good life is not good for us."
-David Satcher, M.D., Ph.D. (Satcher 2004)

The life of an entrepreneur can be physically and emotionally taxing on both you and your family. Through the years, I have come to recognize the importance and value of implementing a series of survival skills that help keep me mentally and physically fit, in order to minimize the stress associated with building and running my businesses.

I would not have been able to survive the life of an entrepreneur without music, a good health regiment, laughter, the presence of quiet time, and learning to "say no."

A Common Sense Approach to Staying Healthy

Maintaining your health is critical to being able to overcome and survive the stress filled life of an entrepreneur. When you consider your body, mind, and spirit as a temple of God, you will work harder to keep it cleansed and fine-tuned.

More and more we are faced with statistics that demonstrate the health effects of certain diets, especially among African-Americans, and other minorities. Many of us have already dealt with the loss of a friend, or loved one due to stress—complicated by diseases associated with our basic lifestyles.

As you begin pursuing the lifestyle of an entrepreneur, I urge you to prepare mentally and physically for the challenge. Start by assessing your risk for any serious health problems. See your physician regularly to address any immediate health issues. Get assistance and guidance on any lifestyle changes necessary to maintain a strong, healthy body.

Keep in mind the old adage, "garbage in—garbage out." To fuel your body with the wrong type of food and exercise, is to clog your mind (and arteries) with unnecessary elements that affect your health and longevity.

According to Dr. James Gavin, III (past President of Morehouse School of Medicine), a few of his "common sense," activities for staying healthy include:

- Take a 30-minute walk every day.
- Eat at least three vegetables and two fruits everyday.
- Drink 6 to 8 glasses of water everyday. More if you play hard and sweat a lot.
- Smile, and smile often.
- Stop smoking.

- Eat good food.
- Get enough sleep
- Find the right place and right fit for God and worship in your life.
- Focus on wellness, not illness.
- Figure out how to lighten your heart, and laugh more often.
- Most important, enjoy life—good food, good conversation, good people, and good music.(Gavin 2004)

For me, staying healthy and physically fit means:

- Good healthy eating habits (no salt, no fatty foods, no pork, limited beef, or no saturated fatty foods) – regular diet of green leafy vegetables and fruits, monitoring the volume of food consumed, and staying away from fast foods when away from home due to meetings, long hours, or travel.
- Avoiding consumption of caffeinated drinks, coffees, or teas. (I find a cup of hot water and lemon helps to calm the body and nerves).
- Physical exercise—a daily workout of some activity you love (walking, running, jogging, swimming, basketball, tennis, etc.)
- Physical exams – annual physical exams, including prostate (for men), all blood work, EKG's, etc.
- Dental Care—annual preventive dental care to assess, maintain and treat any dental health issues that may arise. Many people do not realize the risks associated with abscesses (cause by infection) in the mouth or gums, or periodontal disease.

- Enough sleep (minimum of 6 – 8 hours) daily, along with therapeutic breaks—travel, vacations with family, and scheduled "down time."
- My quiet time with God
- Enjoying life filled with music, laughter, good people, and good conversation.

Music

> *"No other art can inspire and sweeten the personality like music; the lover of music attains sooner or later to the most sublime field of thought."*
>
> Hazrat Inyat Khan (Khan 2005)

Music is known to be a universal language. Through the years, I have gained a greater appreciation of the value and importance for the role music has played in my life. For me, music has become my path to an oasis filled with peaceful and creative thought.

I was introduced years ago to a passage from the Sufi Messages on The Mysticism of Music, Sound, and Word by a creative show director who would ultimately help me expand the scope and vision of my Gospel Choice Awards venture. The Sufi Messages on the Mysticism of Music, Sound, and Word offers tremendous spiritual insight in the value and importance of music in my life:

> When we pay attention to nature's music, we find that everything on the earth contributes to its harmony… spiritualists who have really sounded the depths of spiritualism have realized that there is no better means of attracting the spirits from their plane of freedom to the outer plane than by mu-

sic. They make use of different instruments, which appeal to certain spirits, and sing songs that have a special effect upon the particular spirit with whom they wish to communicate. There is no magic like music for making an effect upon the human soul.

> The effect of music…upon the listener is in accordance with his knowledge and evolution; for this reason the value of music differs with each individual. For a self-satisfied person there is no chance of progress, because he clings contentedly to his taste according to his state of evolution, refusing to advance a step higher than his present level. He who gradually progresses along the path of music, in the end attains to the highest perfection. No other art can inspire and sweeten the personality like music; the lover of music attains sooner or later to the most sublime field of thought. (Khan 2005)

Over the years, I have spent a great deal of time listening to music, in particular that within the spiritual and gospel genres. In the midst of the trials and tribulations of entrepreneurship, music has enabled me to attain levels of tranquility that have become platforms for orchestrating my thought patterns and generating my highest levels of creativity. It is the place where I have found the many answers to questions raised as I wondered through life feeling my sense of God's gifts and talents.

According to the Sufi Messages, "The music of life shows its melody and harmony in our daily experiences. Every spoken word is either a true or a false note, according to the scale of our ideal. The tone of one personality is hard like a horn; while the tone of another is soft like the high notes of a flute." It is no surprise that I have often used music to play the role of counselor in helping to calm the fears and anxieties I've faced at home and in business during my journey as an entrepreneur. It is why I have learned to turn off and tune out the sounds (and imagery) of the "bad news" so often depicted on TV, radio, and other information sources—sounds and imagery that feed negativity into your spirit and soul, disrupting the tranquility needed for creative thinking and business building.

If, according to the Sufi Message, "...the gradual progress of all creation from a lower to a higher evolution...is shown as in music where...the friendship and enmity among men, and their likes and dislikes, are as chords and discords...the human tendency to attraction and repulsion, are like the effect of the consonant and dissonant intervals in music," then it is reasonable to consider that the effect of music upon the developing and established entrepreneur can be profound.

The daily life of an entrepreneur is filled with "all kinds of noise" that comes with the stress of business and personal related economic, financial, and family goals and obligations. To think clearly and respond effectively, one must always find inner peace and tranquility to find and hear the answers needed. Again, I have found listening to commercial free radio at night helps to calm my mind and spirit enough to face each new day with a positive outlook.

As you attain various levels of success in business, I would encourage you to invest in and further broaden your exposure to all types of music artistry and music genres (including Rock 'N Roll, Soul, Classical, Gospel, Spiritual, Spoken Word, etc.). Each one demonstrates the spirit, the lifestyle, the story, the soul, the emotion, etc. of what might just be a potential target consumer, supplier, or collaborator in your business venture. Each one will help you find a greater understanding and awareness of who you really are—and lead you to the outlets in life that will become your personal channels for escape to those tranquil and peaceful oasis necessary for your own creative thinking.

Music became more than just a necessity and driving force for finding my own peace of mind. It was my love of and inspiration from Gospel Music, along with my hairstylist whispering in my ear with every haircut that, "....we need to have a way to celebrate the wonderful gospel artists living right here in Atlanta," and the approving voice of my spirit guide, that became my catalyst and source for creating two successful and growing business ventures—the Annual Gospel Choice Awards (now in its 15th year), followed by the Youth Gospel Choice Awards (sparked by the ever growing Holy Hip-Hop market).

Through the use of my own media outlets and advances in online web applications, I have been able share the power of God's word through music with thousands. I am able to offer the testimonies of wonderful gospel artists via television, streaming faith online video, radio, magazine, and newspaper coverage, and more.

I have turned something I love and am passionate about into a venture that has benefited hundreds and given pleasure to thousands. You too, can do the same!

Quiet Time

"My 3 o'clock AM discussion with God is the most important time in my daily walk through life. It is probably the quietest time for reflection without interference from known and unknown obstacles. It is during that quiet peace when God speaks to me, as I seek the answers to problems and relationships that I have called upon Him for help."
                                                              Creed Pannell, Jr.

One of the most important and often difficult activities that you **must** schedule as an entrepreneur is finding quiet time to reflect upon and contemplate personal and business decisions. Just as children are often requested "take a time out," we must commit to taking a daily "time out" with God to gather our thoughts, reflect, and consider our current situations and actions, or contemplate new ones.

It is during this most important quiet time that you should seek and find answers for the many critical decisions that you will make as an entrepreneur, a business leader, a role model, a parent, a mate, etc. Your quiet time with God is the perfect time to seek help and find the answers for important decisions, such as:

- Are you making the best decision relative to a business partner or mate?
- Are you making a sound business decision regarding your choice for a business location?
- Am I making a good financial or investment decision?
- How will a business decision affect my family and the quality and quantity of time I spend with them?
- What affect will a business decision have on my private and personal time for volunteering or keeping in touch with those close to me?
- How will my decision affect the welfare of my health and physical being?
- What affect will my decision have on my ability to maintain a strong spiritual connection and interaction with my spiritual advisor, church family and leadership, etc? Will it come between my ability to participate in Bible study or Sunday worship?

Should your business venture place you in a leadership role responsible for the livelihood and success of others, your quiet time with God is the time to seek guidance on becoming a good leader and advice on leadership decisions you must make. You will often find yourself seeking answers concerning:

- Your role, for example, as president of a group, organization, or your business.

- How your decisions will affect the quality of life and ultimate performance of those who rely or depend on me—your family and/or those who work with you?

Often times, it might feel like you are all alone on the path you have chosen. But, if you make a daily commitment to honor "your quiet time with God" for discussion and contemplation of your game plan or ideas, you will discover you are never alone. Soon, your quiet time will become your most important ally—for creativity, decision making, and reflection.

Learn to Laugh

Laughter is an absolute "must" in life. If you can't laugh, you become a bore. If you can't laugh, you don't allow yourself an outlet for releasing stress. Laughter allows the entire body to exercise and release unknown toxins in the body.

Life is too short to go through it without being able to laugh at yourself, or with others in social, private, business, personal, or family situations. Laughter provides an outlet for demonstrating the "human" side of you. Laughter is a way of turning negative emotions into positive outlooks.

We know that people and situations (including mistakes) can be funny. After all, that's how comedians make a fortune—finding the humor in the basic things or behaviors we demonstrate everyday in life, while often revealing characteristics among all of us that might need changing. Laughter also helps to ease the tension that can arise during difficult or challenging events in the life an entrepreneur.

Hobbies – Releasing Energy

Hobbies are not just for the young. It is important, as we grow older, to find one or more programs or activities that will aid in your ability to maintain a balanced and healthy life. For some people, it can be learning to play an instrument, painting, singing, sewing, crossword puzzles, playing chess, fixing up or building things around the house, or simply reading for pleasure.

Whatever you do, choose an activity or activities that provide you a means to reduce or release the stress and tension that you will often feel as an entrepreneur. Develop a schedule and routine that includes time to participate and enjoy the hobbies you love.

Remember, you don't have to engage in your hobbies alone. Consider selecting one or two that you might enjoy with other family members, such as running, jogging, or walking. If you like working with your hands or building things, find a time that you might engage in your hobby by volunteering sometime to help build a home with Habitat for Humanity. If you like to play chess, find a chess club for youth and spend some time reaching out and coaching youth. I call that time management—being able to give back to others, releasing stress, and enjoying a game you love all at the same!

Saying "No" to Drugs or Alcoholism

Throughout life, as well as in business, one encounters positive and negative situations that cause many individuals to seek external sources to "ease the pain of life and business decisions." When alcohol or drugs become the mechanisms for celebrating accomplishments and success, or hiding the emotions resulting from failure, one needs to stop and take heed immediately.

Seek out the proper professionals that can help you understand what leads to your frustration levels. What are other mechanisms for coping? Do you have what it takes overcome these issues? Will you be able to cope without the use of drugs or alcohol?

If not, you will be on a pathway to destruction of your business, and your dreams due to poor leadership and decision making errors. More importantly, the use of alcohol and drugs leads to poor judgment that may have significant impact on your employees, as well as your family—those that depend on you.

Through the years, several of my business associates lost sight of their goals and objectives as they leaned over an empty glass of Jack, pondered their next business decision, and asked for another during a business meeting at a local business club. I drank my hot tea with lemon and prayed for them. They would ultimately lose their business, and their family. And, I would pray for them again.

Remember, it is your business and your family. You created these entities to help fulfill your dreams. You must work to avoid all outside and external influences that can tear down your dreams, your goals, and life objectives.

Chapter 6

It's Your Move!

"Success in business requires training and discipline and hard work. But if you're not frightened by these things, the opportunities are just as great today as they ever were."
- David M. Ogilvy (Ogilvy 1994-2007)

Before we get started, I must reiterate that I am firmly convinced it was a Divine calling that led me to join the "entrepreneur's club." I have faith that God will always be there—to help direct my decision-making, clarify my visions, and provide for me during the difficult times.

There are statistics showing that people who are generally considered elite "are less religious in thinking and in practice than are small business owners...that only members of the military and professional athletes are more religious than business owners. Those of us who have started a business and run one today may think everyone in the country thinks like we do, but it just isn't so...we are running our businesses everyday and praying that God will bless us." (Novak n.d.)

Our faith and understanding of God's word teaches us "To those of us who have been given much, much is required." For me, this means that when you have the ideas and energy, you are obligated to use your talents to do something that will help in others. For a business owner, this means helping others develop themselves through employment, earning, and learning.

So you are thinking about becoming an entrepreneur. You have questions about how to get started—how do you decide what business to go into, do you have what it takes, what will it take to become successful, do you have the money to go out on your own, or what do you do if you fail?

First, let us take the option of failure off the table. As Jesus said, "...Invoke the Father, implore God often, and he will give to you. Blessed is he who has seen you with Him when He was proclaimed among the angels, and glorified among the saints; yours is life." Or as Chris Widener, a popular motivational speaker and author would tell you, "Trust in the Lord and go to the hole."

Now that we have that out the way, let us move on to consider some other important factors. Why do you want to be an entrepreneur? Is this the right time for you? Do you have what it takes to be an entrepreneur? Can you do it?

To answer these questions, there is no time like the present to begin talking it over with God. That's right; it's time for you to do a little soul searching. Or, as preachers are often heard saying when they are searching for the sermon to deliver on Sunday, "It's time to go to the "water closet." As you contemplate these, try not to sell yourself short; and open your heart, mind, and soul to what God would have you do.

To help you get started, here are a few ideas I think important for you to consider:

Is entrepreneurship right for you?

Has the idea of becoming an entrepreneur been stirring in your mind. Is it because "you really want it," and feel unfulfilled in your current job; or is it just a backup consideration should you be laid off from your current place of employment

Many people go through much of their adult lives feeling unfulfilled in their daily life— at work, at home, and at play. For the most part, they settle for the "status quo" because— it seems easier, I have a house note or car note to pay, everyone will think I'm crazy, I don't know where or how to begin, I don't have the money, I'm afraid I might not succeed, or I simply don't understand what it is I feel is missing. They go on settling, waiting for the "right time, all the resources, or everything to be in place."

Just imagine how empty many of our lives would be if we waited for the right time, all the resources, and everything to be in place before we started our families? Funny how God often has a different plan in mind?

Perhaps, you should ask yourself a few questions as it relates to understanding your passion and purpose in life, and as an entrepreneur:

Passion—"emotion ...*plural*: the emotions as distinguished from reason: intense, driving, or overmastering feeling or conviction... ardent affection...a strong liking or desire for or devotion to some activity, object, or concept... an object of desire or deep interest." (Passion 2009)

What are you passionate about in life, society, community, etc.? Have you ever had an urge—a passion—to build a race car, find a solution to homelessness, open a retail store, improve upon the early-learning education your children experienced, or spend more time motivating today's youth?

Purpose—"something set up as an object or end to be attained." (Purpose 2009)

If you believe God's purpose for all of us is to love one another, care for one another, and help those in need, is it possible you may be questioning your ability to serve Him, given your current work environment or schedule? Or, perhaps are you sensing there is more for you to accomplish in life?

For those of you that are spiritually grounded, or seeking a greater understanding of God's plan and purpose for you, you might find that what you are simply lacking is the sense of gratification and fulfillment that comes from doing God's work and the work He intended for you.

My source of joy and satisfaction in my work, home, or social life has been deeply rooted in my inner passions, and desire to find God's purpose for me in life. I know that it has been my passion and belief in the economic development of the African-American community through business ownership, and my sense of fulfillment that has motivated me throughout my journey as an entrepreneur.

What resources do you need?

According to Chris Widener, a well known motivational speaker:

> "When people think about pursuing something, they usually first take a look at their resources to determine whether they can do it. That is a wise thing to do.
>
> But where most people fail in this process is when they look at their resources to determine whether or not they can do it, they are usually taking stock of the wrong resources.
>
> Most people immediately look at money. 'How much money do I have?' they ask. Sure, we need to know how much money we have, but money is not the greatest resource. In fact, there are a few other resources that are all more important, and certainly more impacting than money." (Widener n.d.)

As you assess your passion(s) and contemplate your purpose, consider:

> **How much do you want it?** Is it something you have longed for? Is it a burning desire that never ceases? Is it what you believe to be your destiny? If so, have faith and believe that you can and will achieve it!

Are you a person of **vision**, capable of having "...a thought, concept, or object formed by the imagination...the act or power of imagination...mode of seeing or conceiving...unusual discernment or foresight" (Vision 2009), as it relates to what you want to do or be? Now is not the time to worry about the money that may go with the vision—if you can see it, and share it with others, the money will come along?

Can you be **persistent**, able to "go on resolutely or stubbornly in spite of opposition, importunity, or warning?" (Persist 2009) Will you quit if the journey gets rough? Do you have faith enough to believe that all things happen, and will happen, in God's time?

Do you have the **courage**—"mental or moral strength to venture, persevere, and withstand...fear, or difficulty" (Courage 2009)—to trust in God, and believe in the talents and gifts he has given to you?

In the final analysis, if you have all these characteristics, you already possess some of the greatest resources needed to step out into the business world on your own. However, before you take another step, be sure to share your thinking with your spouse, your family, and any others close to you.

Your next step, is to contemplate how much you are willing (or able to give up) to become an entrepreneur. Generally, there are two types of entrepreneurs–those that start out on a full-time basis by learning a business from soup to nuts; and those that start out on a part-time basis while retaining their day jobs and working nights and weekends to develop a customer base of support before becoming full-time professional entrepreneurs.

Now, do you have one "Big" vision, or several? In today's world, I would be classified as a "serial entrepreneur"; and have continued to start-up new ventures through the years, based on the multiple dreams and visions I have had. My start-up of one venture has not always been based upon the success of another, but simply on my desire to satisfy another purpose, one that God had planned for me.

In fact, I have always had a passion, and the belief that minority communities and consumers should be able to have and make choices about goods and services from among African-American (and other ethnic or gender groups) owned enterprises. One of my visions is that we will one day be able to become "players" within the commodities industry segment.

Several years ago, I partnered with a couple of business and religious leaders and founded It's YourChoice Natural Gas. Our strategy, a good strategy, was to collaborate with a significant "up and coming" minority-owned player to provide natural gas services specifically targeted towards the African-American community. We created a giveback promotion that enabled churches, Faith-based and non-profit groups to receive a percentage of their bill in credits or cash donation to help further their outreach and operations.

Our program and strategy was well received. Unfortunately, the market collapse in 2008 disrupted our access to commodity financing for natural gas resources. Our venture was closed due to unpredictable market circumstances. Our vision of providing choices to the African-American community is only deferred.

You may decide, however, that you simply want to start-up or acquire a single entrepreneurial firm or franchise that represents the one "Big" vision, passion, or purpose you are driven by.

Keep in mind, your entrepreneur ventures do not always have to be for-profit concepts. On the other hand, if your goal is simply to go into business on your own in order to maintain a certain lifestyle (a Lifestyle Enterprise), then you will have to determine what type of business suits your wants and needs.

The final decision is up to you. Remember to do your homework, and above all—pray on it!

Preparing To Enter the Game of Entrepreneurship!

This book is not intended to be a technical guide to "Starting Your Own Business." I will leave that to the many experts who have already written and published a multitude of guides to assist in business planning, franchising, capitalizing your business, legal and tax forms for starting a business, marketing and advertising for small businesses, communication tools for small businesses, and more.

I do want to offer you, however, some solid advice based upon the knowledge gained through the trials and errors, media expertise, sales and marketing efforts, quality of customer service, and business management lessons learned and associated with starting more than 10 business ventures in 30 years. Before, and during the process of starting your business, there are lists of important items you must remember **TO DO** and **NOT DO**:

Personal Considerations

- **DO** get your own personal finances in order— determine your bottom line needs to contribute to or maintain your household and basic living expenses. If feasible, set aside enough to sustain (at a minimum) your contribution to your household expenses (including any medical or life insurance policies) through the planning and capitalization of your business; and seek to be able to finance the first six to 12 months of operating expenses for your business (once determined).

- **DO** clean up your credit rating or score (if necessary) as this can aid or hinder your ability to get financing on your own.

- **DO** communicate your plans and intent to "go out on your own" with your family, and friends to gain their support and understanding

- **DO** begin to establish or reestablish a good relationship with your banker, a commercial lender, and/or venture capitalist.

- At a minimum, **DO** invest in the initial purchase of one state-of-the art computer (with an office suite of software applications designed for small businesses), printer and a DSL or broadband connection for your company (to perform online research, document transmission between you and your advisors, etc.). This will minimize the need for transferring some of your business data, documents, etc. upon start-up.

Strategic Business Considerations

Once you identify your passion, and a business vision that will help fulfill your life's purpose, you will need to focus on finalizing your business concept. Given the state of today's economy, shifts in the demographic population, and the trending towards a more global marketplace, it is critical that you employ certain strategic "thinking" in finalizing your business concept and planning process:

- **DO** review trends relative to the fastest growing industries over the past 5 years, and the projected growth industries over the next 5 – to 10 years.

- **DO** take time to become familiar with the government's current, new, and future plans for assisting in the survival, and the development and growth of small businesses. Pay particular attention to the potential availability and access to funding for smaller businesses and job creation, and priorities for recovery (including health, education, economic development for communities, welfare of the people, and technological advancements). Identification of these priorities may represent and signal greater opportunities for capitalizing your business venture.

- **DO** research the nature and priorities for government-funded grants, as it relates to potential opportunities for collaborations with the public or non-profit sector to develop job opportunities or skills among the unemployed and underutilized workforce. (While these grants may require or represent additional reporting, they represent opportunities to support and fund certain lower level staffing requirements you might have.)

- **DO** gain a thorough understanding of the use of technology—specifically the internet, and its relationship to doing business and transmitting information.

- **DO** consider the use and growth of "Virtual" businesses or business practices as a mechanism for reducing operating expenses, managing information flow, and sales between customers, businesses, and suppliers.

- **DO** consider the trend towards development of "Green" businesses, products, and services—as there will most likely be an increase in funding or tax related benefits for working to improve and reduce the impact of global warming.

- **DO** consider opportunities to provide products or services for the increasing number of companies that are outsourcing jobs such as telemarketing, customer service, technical support, etc.

- **DO** assess the needs of your potential customer base that may or may not be met within your community, local or regional marketplace—for example, how can you help improve upon the level of customer service, or provide more cost effective and efficient means to purchase or obtain information given the high cost of gas and oil?

- **DO** take time to study how other cultures, ethnic groups, and/or countries have penetrated and developed successful business enterprises within certain industry segments—parking lots, convenience stores, gas stations, etc.?

- **DO** consider business models that can incorporate for-profit and not-for-profit entities. Such models offer the opportunity for you to address your business and community service passions and goals all in one.

Business Advisors

Throughout your life as an entrepreneur, you will need to rely on and depend upon the advice of professional service consultants that will play a tremendous role in the overall success of your business.

- **DO** take the time to interview several independent consultants or business firms that provide legal, tax, accounting, and financial planning services. Give preference to those who specialize in or have experience within your chosen industry segment.

- **DO** share your thoughts about your vision; as well as your personal, professional, and business goals and objectives. Seek to assess their ability to understand and be compassionate about your goals and objectives, passions, purpose and vision.

- **DO** request references that you can interview before making a decision.

- **DO NOT** make decisions based upon cost alone.

- **DO** take into account "your spirit and gut" feeling about the potential relationship you are about to enter into. I believe that it is always a **good idea** to seek advisors that are also spiritually grounded, and willing to provide advice and recommendations that will enhance your success, and are in keeping with your overall personal, professional, and business goals.

- **DO NOT** enter into a relationship with consultants that operate primarily as "Yes men (or women)".

Business Development and Planning

- **DO** your homework—research your market place, prospective industry segments, customer profile, etc.
- Be sure to read everything you can about your prospective business, study the success rates, and growth trends, and opportunities.
- Subscribe to publications relative to entrepreneurship, your business or industry segment, and your B2B or consumer market.
- **DO** attend and participate in networking activities relative to your business goals and objectives (before, during, after your business planning and launch) **DO** utilize these opportunities to start building a database of customers, potential suppliers, etc.
- **DO** develop a short-term, and long-term (3 year) business plan(including detailed operations and marketing budgets) to serve as your guide and provide a mechanism for tracking your accomplishments, etc. (If you are not experienced with the business planning process, there are many software packages available that will guide you through this process. If funding is available, you may consider hiring a consultant to assist you in this endeavor.)
- **DO** remember to include the development (or inclusion) of a detailed marketing/communications plan to go along with your business plan. (If you are able, seek out the advice of marketing specialists to assist you.) Make sure to:

    Clearly define your target audience or customer base within your desired geographic service area. Understand the changes in demography given your business, products, or services within your desired geographic service area.

Become fully aware of the needs of your customers.

Keep in mind that customer service is the primary key to the success of entrepreneurs, and the sustaining of your business. Begin to determine a game plan for providing customer service that "keeps them coming back," and "willing to promote your business, products, or services to others."

Remember "first impressions are lasting impressions"—be sure to include in your marketing/communications plan budget, costs associated with the "professional" creation, development, and production of your corporate or business identity (i.e., logo, stationary, business cards, etc.); as well as promotional costs associated with the Grand Opening and/or Launch of your business venture including, but not limited to:

- Website (including creative development of a professional site, monthly hosting fees, etc.) **DO** remember, websites are a "must" in today's business environment. As a consumer grows more and more comfortable with on-line shopping, small businesses will search for more cost-effective ways to do business. The need for web sites, ecommerce sites, varieties of internet search engines, pay-for-performance ads, and mobile marketing will grow.

- Media costs (i.e., newspaper, magazine, etc.) Collateral costs (i.e., promotional flyers, signage, brochures, sales materials, product catalogs, etc.)

- Public and Consumer Relations (plan to hire a consultant to help create a media or press kit for your company, and to develop and execute promotional ideas and obtain

PSA—free—publicity, where possible)

- **DO** seek the input of your financial planner, accountant, tax attorney, and banker in the preparation of all your financial worksheets, and projections that will be included in your final business/marketing/communications plan.

- **DO** make sure to include financial consideration for protecting yourself and any employees relative to healthcare and medical insurance, savings, etc.

- **DO** remember to purchase and study materials on Basic Accounting Principles (if you have no accounting or financial planning experience), so that you will able to better understand the financial aspects of running your own business, and the financial reports generated by your internal accounting system (or your accountant)

Operations and Start-up

Once you finalized your business, marketing, and communications plans, seek the advice of your legal, tax, and financial advisors to identify the best organizational structure for your business venture. Have all pertinent documents completed and submitted for the registering your business, obtaining tax ID numbers, and pertinent business licenses required for establishing and operating your business.

Set up any necessary accounts that will enable you to keep your business and personal accounts separate:

- Commercial bank accounts
- Business telephone, internet, fax service, email address, etc.
- Office space (if business is not home-based

- Purchase and/or lease required office equipment (computers, phone system, etc.) to get started, as well as a minimum quantity of office supplies, etc.

Remember to identify and establish initial policies for handling payroll, managing, and tracking accounts receivables, sales, and accounts payables. This will allow you to have systems in place before staffing up, and incurring business expenses.

If you need to raise capital for your business, follow the advice of your banker, commercial loan officer, accountant, etc. for obtaining necessary funding to support your operations, production, or service needs. Always seek the minimum level of capital needed to operate. Do not extend the financial obligations of your business any more than necessary. Remember, any required debt repayments will increase the revenues required to be profitable.

Once you're in business (no matter how small or large), here are a few basic "tidbits" to remember:

- If applicable, always make sure that you can and **DO** pay your permanent employees or sub-contracted consultants or staff on time, according to your pay schedule or agreed upon contracts. (Your accountant should be able to provide insight into setting up these policies or practices.)
- **DO** stay on top of payroll and business taxes that are due. The IRS can become the bane of your existence, if you do not.
- **DO** manage your business expenditures, such that you can always pay your suppliers, and vendors. Without goods and services to operate your business—you cannot stay in business!
- **DO NOT** expect to be profitable overnight.

- **DO** remember that satisfied customers are the most important criteria to success. After all, they are why you are in business!
- **DO** work and follow the business and financial plans you have developed.
- **DO** remember to track and monitor your business, sales, and financial goals, and objectives on a monthly, quarterly, semi-annual, and annual basis.
  Be prepared to adjust your projections and plans as necessary to remain in business, and plan for growth. The worst thing you can do is do nothing.
- **DO NOT** be afraid to step back and "reinvent yourself" if the need arises! If you have been willing to go against the norm by becoming an entrepreneur, then you must be willing to repackage yourself, your business, or your products and services as you grow. You must keep your ideas "fresh," for the sake of your own sanity and development, and that of your customers. In the retail world, for example, the reinvention and product extension of consumable goods equates to the creation of "fads or the latest trends" in electronics, jeans, sneakers, online social networks, etc. They are not necessarily new products, but products that have been repackaged or updated to capitalize on technological advancements, or to meet and create consumer demand among emerging or aging consumer markets. The need to reinvent yourself or your business ideas will be essential to maintaining the momentum required to strive for the best, and to eliminate complacent satisfaction where you are. It is essential to continuing the quest of finding yourself—you are never too old, or too successful to grow and learn.

- **DO** rely on the personal survival skills we've talked about to keep you inspired, focused, and balanced.

Your Business Mortality

As you develop your business, remember to begin a spiritual dialogue with your family regarding the feasibility and desire to continue your business through the next generation of family members or successors. The key to that will be incorporating a means to provide for coverage of the business until obtaining the presence and stability of a key successor. According to Gregory Boop, an experienced business trial lawyer and authorized OSHA trainer:

You should consider 'Key Man' coverage as a part of your business insurance program. Specifically, you should consider the coverage when any of the following apply to your business:

- Your business is a professional services business and key employees cannot be replaced expeditiously because of legal or ethical restraints. For example, a law firm or medical office cannot replace a twenty-year veteran with a new graduate. (Boop NA)

- The business cannot continue in the event of a loss of particular people. Imagine "The Dog Whisperer" without Cesar Millan. The fact is that some businesses are simply not a business without a particular person in the operation. (Boop NA)

- Business continuity is a concern. Look at your partner's children, your wife, and other heirs. Do they know the business? Do they care? Are they in the same profession? Your partner's share of the business will be inherited by someone and the business may need to buy out that person's share or dissolve the business. (Boop NA)

- Future growth or financing is possible. Most financiers and banks will require this coverage to be in place before extending any financing or credit to the company. If the company merges or goes public, this coverage will be required on top executives and board members. (Boop NA)
- The key persons are between the ages of 30 and 55. Young key people are more likely to be disabled than die. Young key people are also the least likely to have adequately planned for their death. Thus, if your business has young key people consider this coverage because it is human nature for young people to ignore their mortality and the business may be hurt by the lack of planning. (Boop NA)

"The cost of this coverage can often be defrayed as a business expense on company taxes (see your tax professional). The cost is often cheaper because it is sold as a term product usually for fifteen to twenty years and often corresponding to the most productive work years of the employee or officer. Your company may not need this coverage, but even engaging in the analysis of whether this coverage is necessary is often helpful. Do the analysis and consider what you would if Employee X was not able to work tomorrow." (Boop NA)

The Future of Entrepreneurship

I am excited about the future possibilities for entrepreneurship, both nationally, and globally. There is no argument—entrepreneurship aids in stabilizing and strengthening economies, whether developed, developing, or underdeveloped:

Entrepreneurs create new businesses, generating jobs for themselves and those they employ. In many cases, entrepreneurial activity increases competition and, with technological or operational changes, it can increase productivity as well...

In the United States, for example, small businesses provide approximately 75 percent of the net new jobs added to the American economy each year and represent over 99 percent of all U.S. employers. The small businesses in the United States are often ones created by self-employed entrepreneurs. "Entrepreneurs give security to other people; they are the generators of social welfare," said Carl J. Schramm, president and chief executive officer of Ewing Marion Kauffman Foundation...

Others agree that the benefits of small businesses go beyond income. Hector V. Baretto, administrator of the U.S. Small Business Administration (SBA), explains, "Small businesses broaden the base of participation in society, create jobs, decentralize economic power, and give people a stake in the future.

According to the *2006 Summary Results of the Global Entrepreneurship Monitor (GEM)* project, "Regardless of the level of development and firm size, entrepreneurial behavior remains a crucial engine of innovation and growth for the economy and for individual companies since, by definition, it implies attention and willingness to take advantage of unexploited opportunities." (Holden 2008)

In spite of more immediate predictions of foreclosure, and bankruptcy among small businesses, there is agreement that entrepreneurs will play a vital role in "mobilizing resources and promoting economic growth and socio-economic development. This is particularly true in the developing world, where successful small businesses are primary engines of job creation and poverty reduction." (Holden 2008)

Layoffs, among major employers and small businesses are expected to continue well into 2011, and possibly beyond. Millions of newly and currently unemployed will begin to contemplate starting their own businesses. Although it is expected that financing for new start-up business will be illusive for a while, it will be important to consider opportunities that may be generated given projected increases in federal funding to expand broadband access, technological advancements, and the development of "green or clean" environments, etc.

In the meantime, I would be remiss if I did not remind you to be sure to consider your passions, visions, and purpose. For the past couple of decades, there has been an "explosion of entrepreneurship and a healthy competition in the social sector…This revolution [called Social Entrepreneurship] is fundamentally changing the way society organizes itself and the way we approach social problems…bringing electricity, water, medicine and other life-changing tools and resources to people in the developing world." (PBS 2005)

Whether considering entrepreneurship by choice or by layoff, it may be good time to consider that perhaps God has a different master plan. "There are religions which take the view that God resides in all of nature. For example, "Jews and Christians believe…that we are called to be 'co-creators with God' and that God gives us the ability to think of new ways to solve problems. If people need to get from one side of the mountain to the other, we think, let's build a road. We don't think, well, we'll just have to do without going to the other side of the mountain." (Novak n.d.) Social Entrepreneurs are helping to rebuild economies, and relationships throughout the world. Stephen Ambrose, an agnostic, wrote in his book, Nothing Like It in the World, "about the strong faith held by the entrepreneurs who saw in their mind's eye a railroad crossing this country. These men put their hard-earned money and their lives on the line to make it happen. Ambrose quoted an American engineer as saying, "Where a mule can go, I can make a locomotive go." Ambrose concluded that the project was too hard and too scary to do without the leaders' belief that God was with them." (Novak n.d.)

Think about it! What would you do if you felt God had called on you to do something special?

What is Social Entrepreneurship?

"Social entrepreneurs identify resources where people only see problems. They view the villagers as the solution, not the passive beneficiary. They begin with the assumption of competence and unleash resources in the communities they're serving."
David Bornstein, author of How to Change the World: Social Entrepreneurs and the Power of New Ideas (PBS 2005)

Social entrepreneurship, by definition, is the work of a social entrepreneur—a change agent, one who benefits humanity through innovations and innovative business concepts. "This need not be incompatible with making a profit - but social enterprises are often non-profits. Social enterprises are for 'more-than-profit' (a term coined by a BBC journalist)." (Wikipedia contributors n.d.)

President Obama's Economic Recovery and Urban Policy agendas include priorities for increasing funding for small business incubators, public and private partnerships, as well as faith-based and neighborhood partnerships. The impetus for such funding is great—we are **all** responsible for the redevelopment and revitalization of our economy (locally, nationally, as well as globally).

"Whether...working on a local or international scale, social entrepreneurs share a commitment to pioneering innovation that reshape society and benefit humanity...they are solution-minded pragmatists who are not afraid to tackle some of the world's biggest problems." (Skoll Foundation n.d.) If you have a desire to have a positive impact on the lives of the marginalized and disenfranchised citizens of your community, nation, or the world, social entrepreneurship may be for you.

While I have yet to establish a non-profit organization or social enterprise, I have endeavored to incorporate many of our social ills or injustices through the manifestation of support and awareness that are outcomes of our business ventures. As a result, I have taken the opportunity to use the publications, other media outlets, and branded events (i.e., Georgia Minority Business Awards, Annual Gospel Choice Awards, and the Youth Gospel Choice Awards) to provide recognition, scholarships, and donations to non-profit groups that promote and support causes that I am passionate about: youth entrepreneurship, homelessness, hunger, and economic development.

In whatever you choose to do—be true to yourself, believe in yourself, and above all else—trust in God!

Go for it! It's your move!

Chapter 7

Exploring and Building Strategic Options

> *"The World is a book, and those who do not travel read only a page."*
> —Saint Augustine (Augustine, Brainy Quotes
> -St. Augustine Quote n.d.)

Once you have begun "the entrepreneurship game," it will be important to constantly explore and create options that enable your business to adapt to changes in the marketplace, participate in a more global economy, improve upon your product or service offerings, expand or stretch your vision, and enhance your business skills. In my experience, I have found travel to be not only therapeutic, but to, more importantly, aid in the development of professional, political, and civic networking opportunities that have become essential to my success.

Travel

There are many people who cannot travel for personal or financial reasons. And, there are people who will not travel. Through the years, I have come to appreciate and value the importance of travel in my life and business success.

A young woman growing in her own faith once wrote, "On a journey, you go from place to place to a point of no return. Therefore, journey to a new place in Christ. In Christ, there's new possibilities, new hope, new strength, new faith. Remain open-minded. Open the bible and learn something new everyday and watch your growth." (Scott 2008)

Each trip I take with my family or for business becomes a journey to explore and expand the boundaries of my life, my thinking, and my creativity. By my own faith and understanding, I believe that God calls us to explore every frontier of His greatness and glory.

When you lean on God for His guidance and wisdom in the building of your business ventures, you will soon realize God is always challenging you to turn the page—to leave the comfort and security of your homes, communities, and offices to discover a greater purpose or opportunity (both nationally and internationally) that is destined for you. If travel is not an absolute requirement for your business, then you must commit to utilize vacation time to go on at least one major journey each year.

Given today's global economy, it is more imperative than ever that we journey to new cities, new countries, and new marketplaces so that we can:

- Enhance our business planning.

- Develop strategies for growth and new business opportunities with other cultures.
- Build and increase our understanding of an ever changing, and evolving business environment.
- Identify and develop relationships and business resources for growth and expansion.

Networking

Building a business is no "small task." It should never be attempted in a vacuum. Throughout your business career, you will need to rely upon a network of business associates, friends, mentors, professional advisors, along with public, private, and civic leaders to help you along the way. For some, networking comes easy. For others, the task can be frightening and often overwhelming.

It is critical for an entrepreneur to be able to overcome any fears you may have of meeting people—professionally and socially. You can begin this process by joining and participating in professional organizations for entrepreneurs and those reflective of your particular discipline and industry segment. Most organizations of this nature will provide more immediate access to data, current and projected trends in your chosen field. Associations for entrepreneurs, and other professional and industry related organizations provide:

- Camaraderie and support from members who are experiencing all of the challenges of entrepreneurship that you will face.
- Offer more immediate access to experts and resources that can provide guidance and support in your specific business venture.

Another critical networking opportunity exists through membership and participation in activities of well-known and respected community-based, social, and civic organizations (such as Greek fraternities and sororities, alumni associations, etc.) For small business owners and entrepreneurs, these relationships provide:

- Outlets and opportunities to promote your business, products, or services—usually at no cost or minimal expense.
- Opportunities to grow intellectually, socially, and professionally through the mutual respect and sharing of ideas, and concepts among those with similar, as well as broader interests and perspectives on business, the world, the community, etc.

Keep in mind that how you approach the utilization and development of these networking opportunities, will affect the value and outcome of the relationships you establish. Once again, first impressions can create lasting impressions.

If you are spiritually grounded, and building your business with the understanding of God's purpose for you under His guidance; you will be able to recognize important networking opportunities that have been divinely ordered.

To get the most out of these opportunities, you must be willing to **give** as much as you get. Greater value is gained by establishing mutual respect and appreciation for the contacts you make. Your approach should always be genuine and sincere—you must believe (and act accordingly) that God has ordered this relationship for the mutual benefit and growth of both parties.

I remember the day I was introduced to Mr. Marmmadou Camara from Africa. He was a salesperson for a car dealership that was a primary sponsor of one of my annual events.

As we came to know one another, we both recognized that it was divinely planned that we would meet. My newfound friend had been interested in pursuing the means to create a networking opportunity that would connect and help to provide information for entrepreneurs in his homeland. As a result, I shared the concept and purpose of the GMBA. Further discussions have led to a greater opportunity and purpose for traveling to Africa, while offering guidance and strategies to assist in helping implement his vision for businesses in his country.

Be mindful of your environment and the circumstances surrounding the initial meeting of a contact you have been "waiting, hoping, or praying anxiously to meet." For example, if you are in a social setting or attending a special event, don't attempt to monopolize the individual's time with aggressive efforts to "impress the contact with all your business acumen, goals, and objectives." Use the opportunity to express sincere appreciation for the meeting; identify some mutual ground or interest for establishing interest in developing the relationship further; ask permission to follow up at a later date; and most importantly—follow through!

Your initial contact and follow through will set the tone for future meetings, and help establish a perception of trust, honesty, and sincerity in you as an individual and businessperson. As your relationship develops, always bear in mind that "you never know how many people you are talking to" when engaged in any conversation. Strive to always present and maintain a professional and positive attitude.

Above all, remember to thank God for the opportunity.

Playing the Political Game

It is important for you to get to know the political movers and shakers in your community, city, state, and industry segment. "We may not always recognize it, but government plays a bigger role in our lives than any other single person or institution. We spend nearly half of our lives working to pay for it...every area of our lives feels the influence of government," said Harry Browne of the Libertarian Party.

It is important for you to take an active role in politics. This doesn't mean you have to run for office, but it does mean that you need to be familiar with the political process in the country, and become acquainted with your local state, city, and community government officials.

Find opportunities to meet politicians, especially the local politicians that represent your state, city, and the neighborhoods where you live and do business. When feasible, donate your time and some resources to your favorite political leaders and their campaigns.

Obtaining access to your local politicians, will give you greater insight into and awareness of pending decisions that will be made—decisions that can often affect the way you do business, or provide opportunities that will help maximize your business. For example, government funding may be available in certain communities—designated in the past as Empowerment Zones, or Promise Neighborhoods per President Obama's Urban Policy agenda—to provide incentives to the business and development communities to build and establish businesses (and create jobs), as well as housing in neighborhoods that have been severely underserved. Relationships with political contacts (especially local officials), might also provide insight into pending RFPs for government contracts, or new business ventures coming into the area that may be important to you as an entrepreneur.

Be sure to register as a disadvantaged and/or small business enterprise, once you have established a sound business and financial history. You'll find the SBA (Small Business Administration) a helpful source for developing relationships, and marketing your products and services within the US government. Be sure to take time to research national, state, and local government web sites to gain understanding of the requirements for doing business with government agencies. In all cases, there will be advantages to having registered as a disadvantaged (minority, female, and veteran-owned) business enterprise (if applicable).

While registering with local, city, state, and federal agencies as a small or disadvantage business is a requirement for doing business with government agencies, you must still market yourself and your company. Your political contacts can be helpful to you in directing or introducing you to the purchasing agents and/or decision makers.

One final recommendation for you to consider:

Given the current economic status of our country, the election of President Barack Obama, and the development of Economic Recovery Plan(s) that will affect all levels of society, it is important that you stay abreast of the structuring and use of "bail-out" monies. As the American public has shown, your "voice" for change can make a difference. Therefore, it is becoming more imperative that you express your concerns, and provide input to your local, state, and national government officials as it relates to the availability of funding and opportunities to support start-up ventures and the vitality of entrepreneurship.

Chapter 8

Taking Stock of You

"Success in business requires training and discipline and hard work. But if you're not frightened by these things, the opportunities are just as great today as they ever were."
— David M. Ogilvy (Ogilvy 1994-2007)

How others view you

Perception is everything. As an entrepreneur living in a society too often dominated by the need for status, material wealth, and self-worth, you may find yourself viewed by your peers characteristically as a "low or high maintenance" individual. You will often be judged by the impressions you make among family, friends, and business associates.

In growing up, our parents always emphasized the importance of making good "first impressions," as they can create "lasting impressions" of our character and worth. After all, that's why advertising and public relations experts (Spin Doctors) make a tremendous living by creating and building positive perceptions and imagery for corporate executives, product brands, and services.

Your credibility as a business leader is critical to your growth and ultimate success as an entrepreneur. You will be judged by not only your personal accomplishments or the viability and success of your products or services, but by your accomplishments and contributions to your community and society.

Your strength in character and your commitment to "your word is bond," will greatly influence the perceptions of others. You must always strive to live your life and manage your business ventures with the highest integrity. Remember that:

- When you make commitments, honor them.
- When you rise, lift another up.
- When you make decisions, make them based upon the good of all, not for the good of one!
- When you speak, speak truthfully.
- When you listen, listen sincerely.
- If you must judge, judge quietly.

- If you must criticize, do so softly with words of encouragement.
- When you succeed, thank God!

Honing your skills

While formal education is not explored in this book (nor required to become an entrepreneur), There is great significance and value in having obtained a formal college education (at a minimum); with pertinent courses, workshops, or seminars in entrepreneurship, small business marketing, etc. Small business or entrepreneur related courses would help to keep you updated on trends and issues effecting entrepreneurs. Becoming successful, as an entrepreneur requires an awareness of the changing business climate and understanding of the global marketplace in which we now live.

There is always something new to learn. Formal education and ongoing course enrollment is one way to challenge and stimulate your own abilities to problem solve and make decisions without some of the risk associated with "On the Job Training and Decision Making" within your own venture.

Leadership is earned and defined by the solutions you offer, business decisions you make, and the confidence in your abilities as perceived by others. Continued education and participation in leadership training programs will provide opportunities to meet other corporate, and business people, as well as civic and social leaders. Participation in one of the "premier" programs in your area will provide opportunities to observe and develop strategic planning, and the decision making and thought processes of others who are respected for their leadership and contribution in their industries and communities.

Dealing with Rejection

In business, the one word that you will have to conquer is "NO." One of the greatest obstacles to overcome by prospective and existing entrepreneurs is the fear of failure—the personal fear of rejection of your ideas, thoughts, processes, and organization.

I remember the first time I had a potential customer along my paper route tell me "no, I'm not interested in subscribing to the paper." My first reaction was that it was because I was a "little Black boy." But then, I stepped back and thought about the many relationships that I had been able to establish between people of all races. I was determined not to let that be my reason for failure— for not making the sale. I picked myself up, got back on my bike, and went on to make another sale.

I've learned you must draw upon your faith to gain strength and understanding that the word "NO" does not automatically signal a personal attack or rejection. For me, I have learned to view and accept rejection of my ideas or business proposals as, quite simply, an opportunity that challenges me to improve upon my ideas, and presentations. In sales, you learn that the word "NO" usually indicates an objection that you can and must work to overcome in order to attain success.

When faced with the word "NO," consider:

- Did you make yourself clear in presenting your ideas or proposals? Perhaps you will need to further research or reevaluate your presentation for more viable alternatives or solutions for that prospect.
- Did you seek understanding of your prospects initial decision (i.e., what would it take to make this a viable option

or solution for your business)?

- Was the quality of your presentation materials or proposal professional, and first-class?
- Are your communication and presentation skills effective?
- Was your presentation flawed with incorrect data relative to your prospect?
- Was your prospect the "right" prospect suited for the presentation of your ideas, requests, products, or services?
- Are there any apparent or hidden market changes that could have affected the outcome of your presentation or request?
- Was the timing of your presentation or request "off," given the recipients preoccupation with internal or personal issues?
- Are there any known, or potential conflicts between you and your prospect (and his/or her company)?
- Was your appearance professional, neat, clean, and reflective of your environment at the time?

When faced with rejection, keep in mind that "Nothing beats a failure but a try." Remember that you can't fail unless you try, and if you fail at trying, try again! Never become frustrated or angry when you are told "NO."

Bottom line—be persistent and determined! Turn every obstacle into an opportunity for honing your sales and presentation skills, or for further growing and improving upon ideas, products, or service offerings.

Planning your exit

Whether just starting out as an entrepreneur, or having spent several years as an entrepreneur, it's never too soon to plan for exiting your life as an entrepreneur. If you have been successful, and fulfilled many of your dreams, you will want to look ahead—plan for a future that allows you to enjoy and "reap" the benefits of all that you done and earned.

Here are few "tips" to consider and keep in mind:

- Get some idea as to how long you think you want to play the Game of Entrepreneurship.

- Will your children or other family members be interested in taking over once you retire? (If so, make sure to build in the opportunity for them become engaged in the business early on—or as soon as they are able.)

- Talk with your financial planning and tax advisors about establishing an individual retirement plan for you—including recommended schedules and options for savings, pension, and investments (stocks, bonds, and real estate)—based upon your company salary or withdrawals from your business.

- Always maintain and run your business as if you hope to sell it one day. Stay abreast of trends in business and in your marketplace. Don't let your pride or ego stand in your way. If an "ideal or market driven" opportunity presents itself to sell your business and move on in life, or to another venture, consider it!

> *All my growth and development led me to believe that if you really do the right thing, and if you play by the rules, and if you've got good enough, solid judgment and common sense, that you're going to be able to do whatever you want to do with your life.*
>
> Barbara Jordon (Jordan n.d.)

Chapter 9

The Wisdom of Success!

"Service is the rent we pay to be living. It is the very purpose of life and not something you do in your spare time."

-Marian Wright Edelman
(Edelman, Culture of Peace Initiative:
Quotes for Volunteers 2006)

If you have been blessed by God with the opportunity to successfully pursue and fulfill your dreams (or your "calling"), then you should have the wisdom to know that you did not do it on your own. Therefore, you should feel a sense of obligation and commitment to God to "help others, less fortunate than you."

Service is the price you pay

As you build your business, always plan and structure a committed amount of time for you to help others. What's so difficult about that? Nothing! Remember, there are many individuals who were not fortunate enough to have similar experiences to you, or the same background and support systems as you, or perhaps who simply did not make the same choices in life as you. Some individuals did not know how to pray about opportunities presented to them. More importantly, many individuals may not have heeded God's words, or warnings presented to them in life; and now find themselves in situations that cause us to be reminded, "there for the grace of God, go I."

You might wish to consider developing opportunities within your own business venture to offer paid and unpaid internships for college students to provide first-hand exposure to the life of entrepreneurship. You might seek opportunities to create part-time or full-time work opportunities in conjunction with welfare to work government programs to assist unemployed or underemployed persons seeking to return to the workforce, or develop additional skills. This is a wonderful way to assist families and communities to gain economic stability, increase the purchasing power of potential business consumers or customers, and to enhance the overall quality of life for residents and businesses in your surrounding business locale.

You will find that when you help others, you will receive one of God's greatest gifts—Joy! You will gain a level of personal satisfaction that, surprisingly, often exceeds or is different from that gained by the success of your business. Devoting some amount of time and resources to helping others through your business, as well as outside activities will enhance you as a person, and help keep you grounded relative to your own success.

Importance of Volunteerism

Throughout your life, I expect that there have been social issues and ills that have touched you or your family deeply. Whether it is homelessness, cancer, domestic violence, child abuse, drug abuse, youth, etc., you should begin identifying a cause that you want to support as an individual and/or as a business entity in order to be a part of offering a solution to bring about change in your community.

While supporting organizations financially is always welcomed, volunteering your time and talent allows you to demonstrate your commitment to finding and providing solutions to social and economic issues that plague so many. Through active participation and involvement, you may also be able to further your own business opportunities through meeting many business, civic, and social leaders actively participating in revitalizing and stabilizing the communities they work and live in.

In the words of George Washington Carver, "How far you go in life depends on you being tender with the young, compassionate with the aged, sympathetic with the striving and tolerant of the weak and the strong. Because someday in life you will have been all of these." (Carver n.d.) Some of your greatest rewards will come when you have the chance to help a homeless person or family transition into a home again; inspire young people to become leaders, to excel in school, or pursue higher education; or when you help unemployed or under employed persons gain confidence in their own ability to pursue entrepreneurship or home-based businesses. These rewards will be among some of your greatest personal accomplishments.

If you are not sure where to begin, you might start with participating in outreach programs of your church. To find other organizations to volunteer your time or support, contact your local United Way for a list and description of organizations giving help and needing help throughout your communities, or pay attention to requests for volunteer efforts through your church, the media, the Red Cross, or personal requests of you.

In fact, I did just that. While I was living in a small community in Florida, I was asked if I would be willing to donate some time to serve as a volunteer ambulance driver for a local EMS service in need of a driver, but no budget to support hiring enough drivers to keep the ambulances rolling.

I didn't want to even consider having to call for an ambulance and being told, we'll get someone there as soon as we are able. I did what I thought God would want me to do—I adjusted my busy schedule so that could accommodate their needs during the night time shift, until funding allowed them to hire an additional driver. I was rewarded, more than you know, each time I was able to help get a person to the hospital in time to save a life, deliver a baby, or reach the emergency care they needed.

I have one life and one chance to make it count for something . . . I'm free to choose what that something is, and the something I've chosen is my faith. Now, my faith goes beyond theology and religion and requires considerable work and effort. My faith demands — this is not optional — my faith demands that I do whatever I can, wherever I am, whenever I can, for as long as I can with whatever I have to try to make a difference.

Jimmy Carter (Carter n.d.)

Chapter 10

Keeping Life Simple...

I cannot give you the formula for success, but I can give you the formula for failure, which is: Try to please everybody.
                                Herbert B. Swope (Swope n.d.)

Life can be a beautiful, live timepiece of discovery for everyone. We are all destined by God to become someone special in His eyes. We honor Him, when we actively engage ourselves in activities that demonstrate respect, love, care, and concern for others. Your ultimate success will be determined by how well you lead your life each day as a business person, a mate, a parent, a friend, a mentor, and a faithful servant to God.

While we all have basic survival skills and possess some "street smarts," it may take some time to study and gain understanding of the plans and great gifts God has intended for you. As you grow, you will have choices to make in your life that will affect your lifestyle, relationships, and business decisions. Once you are perceived as a "successful" entrepreneur, business associates, friends, and family may begin to make more demands or your time, resources, etc. Your choices and willingness to try to accommodate others can add confusion (which always leads to more confusion) to your already hectic schedule and ultimately determine how positive or negative the outcomes of your decisions or actions will be. It is incumbent upon you find your "spiritual side" and take the time to discover and study God's plan for your life's journey.

One of the most valuable lessons I have learned while playing the entrepreneur game is—it's okay to say no! I have come to accept that I cannot be all things to all people, and that it is not my sole responsibility to help everyone. I have had to learn to keep my life as simple as possible—in the face of the life of an entrepreneur—if I am to realize God's purpose and plan for me.

Remember with age comes wisdom. The greatest gift you can give yourself is to "Keep Life Simple." The Bible, the Holy Koran, the Torah, etc. are the greatest books of knowledge available to you for seeking understanding and wisdom of The Master's plan for you. All you have to do is—Let go and Let God!

As you travel along your path of entrepreneurship, there will be bumpy roads! I have relied on my faith and belief in God to see me through. I offer these final words of prayer, comfort, and guidance as you set out on *your journey* of a lifetime:

Always remember, God is there.

If you fall, He will lift you up.

When you are weak, He is strong.

When you are lost, He is the way.

When you are hungry, He will feed you.

When you are hurt, He will heal you.

When you stumble, He will steady you.

When you face loss, He will provide for you.

When you face problems, He will comfort you.

Always remember, everyday is a Blessing!

Bibliography

PBS. *What is Social Entrepreneurship?* 2005. http://www.pbs.org/opb/thenewheroes/whatis/index.html (accessed February 9, 2009).

Augustine, Saint. *Brainy Quotes - Saint Augustine Quotes.* ND. http://www.brainyquote.com/quotes/quotes/s/saintaugus108132.html (accessed December 12, 2008).

—. *Brainy Quotes- Saint Augustine Quotes.* ND. http://www.brainyquote.com/quotes/quotes/s/saintaugus105703.html (accessed December 13, 2008).

Boop, Gregory. "Business Insurance: Key Man Insurance." *About.Com (part of The New York Times Company)* . NA. http://businessinsure.about.com/od/typesofpolicies/a/keymanins.htm (accessed February 5, 2009).

Browne, Harry. *Political Quotes.* ND. http://www.newspeakdictionary.com/ot-quotes.html#QPrograms (accessed January 28, 2009).

Buck, Pearl S. *Wisdom Quotes - Pearl S. Buck.* Edited by Jone Johnson Lewis. 1995 - 2009. http://www.wisdomquotes.com/002192.html (accessed December 12, 2008).

Carter, Jimmy. *Wisdom Quotes: Jimmy Carter.* http://www.wisdomquotes.com/000154.html (accessed December 8, 2008).

Carver, George Washinton. *Brainy Quote: George Washington Carver Quotes.* http://www.brainyquote.com/quotes/quotes/g/georgewash106292.html (accessed February 1, 2009).

Courage. 2009. http://www.merriam-webster.com/dictionary/courage (accessed February 5, 2009).

Edelman, Marian Wright. *Culture of Peace Initiative: Quotes for Volunteers.* 2006. http://www.cultureofpeace.org/quotes/volunteer-quotes.htm (accessed December 12, 2008).

—. "Marian Wright Edelman Commencement Speech to the graduating class of Tarbut V'Torah in Irvine, California." *Womens Speech Archive.* May NA, 2004. www.womenspeecharchive.org/files/Marian_Wright_Edelman_Commencement__1193948735897.pdf (accessed January 27, 2009).

Einstein, Albert. Wisdom *Quotes: Albert Einstein.* http://www.wisdomquotes.com/001754.html (accessed December 8, 2008).

Gavin, III (M.D., Ph.D.), James R. *Dr. Gavin's Health Guide for African Americans.* Alexandria, VA: Small Steps Press, 2004.

Holden, Jeanne. "Economics and Trade/Achieving growth through open markets:Entrepreneurship Aids the Economy." *America.gov.* May 12, 2008. http://www.america.gov/st/econ-english/2008/May/20080603233010eaifas0.8230554.html (accessed February 9, 2009).

Jordan, Barbara. *Wisdom Quotes: Barbara Jordan.* http://www.wisdomquotes.com/001881.html (accessed December 8, 2008).

Khan, Hazrat Inayat Khan. "Spiritual Message of Hazrat Inayat Khan: Volume II- The Mysticism of Music, Sound and Word PartI: The Mysticism of Sound Chapter VII Music." *wahiduddin's web.* Checked - October 18, 2005. http://wahiduddin.net/mv2/II/II_7.htm (accessed January 5, 2009).

Moore, Thomas. *Wisdom Quotes: Thomas Moore.* http://www.wisdomquotes.com/001742.html (accessed December 8, 2008).

Novak, Michael. *Online Video Clip Translation: See Ownership As Your Calling.* http://search.smallbusinessschool.org/video.cfm?clip=996 (accessed February 2, 2009).

Ogilvy, David M. *Quotations by Author: David M. Ogilvy.* Edited by Michael Moncur. 1994 -2007. http://www.quotationspage.com/quotes/David_M._Ogilvy/ (accessed December 12, 2008).

Passion. 2009. http://www.merriam-webster.com/dictionary/passion (accessed February 5, 2009).

Persist. 2009. http://www.merriam-webster.com/dictionary/persist (accessed February 5, 2009).

Purpose. 2009. http://www.merriam-webster.com/dictionary/purpose (accessed February 5, 2009).

Satcher, David (M.D., Ph.D.). "Forward." Chap. Forward in *Dr. Gavin's Health Guide for African Americans: How to Keep Yourself and Your Children Well*, by III (M.D., Ph.D), James R. Gavin, v. Alexandria, VA: Small Steps Press, 2004.

Scott, Katina. *Soar Above Medicrity By Living a Bible Life: ABC's to Maintaining Your Joy!* February 14, 2008. http://www.irrefutablewisdom.blogspot.com/ (accessed January 27, 2009).

Skoll Foundation. *Background on Social Entrepreneurship.* http://www.skollfoundation.org/aboutsocialentrepreneurship/index.asp (accessed February 9, 2009).

Some, Sobonfu. *Spirit of Intimacy: Ancient African Teachings in the Ways of Relationships.* New York, NY: Harper Collins Publishers, Inc., 1997.

Swope, Herbert B. *Wisdom Quotes: Herbert B. Swope.* ttp://www.wisdomquotes.com/003210.html (accessed December 8, 2008).

Thoreau, Henry David. *Wisdom Quotes: Henry David Thoreau.* http://www.wisdomquotes.com/000300.html (accessed December 8, 2008).

Vision. 2009. http://www.merriam-webster.com/dictionary/vision (accessed February 5, 2009).

Vistage International, Inc. "Vistage Small Business Program." *Vistage International, Inc. Web site.* http://www.vistage.com/programs/vistage-programs/small-business-program.html (accessed February 5, 2009).

Widener, Chris. "Your Greatest Resources - Motivational Article." *Ascension Gateway Web site.* 2002. http://www.ascensiongateway.com/spiritual-articles/authors/widener/motivational-resources.htm (accessed January 27, 2009).

Wikipedia contributors. *Social entrepreneurship.* http://en.wikipedia.org/w/index.php?title=Social_entrepreneurship&oldid=268963806 (accessed February 9, 2009).

Wikisource contributors. *Meditation XVII by John Donne.* Edited by Wikisource The Free Library. Vers. Page ID: 822389. last revision: November 3, 2008. http://en.wikisource.org/w/index.php?title=Meditation_XVII&oldid=822389 (accessed February 4, 2009).

Index

a

accounting *16, 54, 57*

associations *69, 116*

b

banker *51, 57, 58*

basic accounting principles *14, 19, 25, 36, 39, 52, 56, 57, 69, 84, 108*

business advisors *54*

business expenditures *58*

business identity *56*

business plan *55, 106, 108, 121*

business venture *14, 19, 25, 36, 39, 52, 56, 57, 69, 84, 108*

c

certification *120*

child *17, 18, 85*

children *xii, 2, 3, 4, 5, 17, 18, 19, 20, 38, 46, 61, 80, 125*

comic books *24, 25*

commercial lender *51*

communications *55, 56, 57, 124*

community involvement *xii*

community service *53*

computer *51*

corporate or business identity *56*

courage *48, 92*

creativity *28*

credibility *76*

credit rating or score *51, 100*

customer *6, 7, 8, 48, 50, 53, 55, 56, 78*

customer service *6, 7, 50, 53, 56*

d

dealing with rejection *78*

divine calling *44*

drugs or alcoholism *v, 41*

e

economic recovery *65, 73*

entrepreneurship club *44*

entrepreneurship education *106*

etiquette *xii*

f

faith *xv, 3, 14, 15, 37, 44, 47, 48, 64, 65, 68, 78, 91, 123*

faithful servant *2, 90*

family *ix, xi, xii, xiii, 4, 10, 14, 17, 29, 31, 34, 36, 38, 39, 40, 41, 48, 51, 60, 68, 76, 80, 85, 90, 101, 125*

father *xi, xii, 2, 4, 7, 17, 18, 24*

fatherhood and family *17*

financial goals *59*

financial planning *54, 57, 80*

financial planning services *54*

for-profit *50, 53, 118*

franchise *17, 50, 102, 104, 105, 107*

franchise solutions for women *105*

full-time professional entrepreneurs *48*

future of entrepreneurship *61*

g

game plan *xii, 126, 127, 128*

good manners *xii*

government *120*

h

healthy eating *33*

hobbies *40*

honing your skills *77*

i

impressions *56, 70, 76*

IRS *58*

j

k

key man *60, 92*

l

leadership *28, 77, 111, 112*

legal, tax, accounting

life partner *16*

lifestyle enterprise *50*

m

marketing *2, 9, 16, 50, 55, 56, 57, 73, 77,* 107, *109,* 111, 112, *118, 120, 123, 124*

marketing/communications plan *55, 56, 57*

media *56, 110, 118*

media costs *56*

military and veteran franchises *105*

music *34, 37, 93*

n

networking *55, 67, 69, 70,* 111, *116*

o

objectives *16, 41, 54, 55, 59, 71*

operating expenses *51, 53*

outsourcing *53*

p

passion *46, 93*

perception *76*

persistent

persistence *48, 79*

personal considerations *51*

physically fit *31, 33*

planning *55, 80, 107, 108, 110*

planning your exit *80*

political game *72*

politicians *72*
politicians *72*

projected growth industries *52*

promotional costs *56*

public and consumer relations *56*

publications *55*

purpose *46, 94*

q

quiet time *37*

r

reinvent yourself *59*

rejection *78*

research *51, 52, 55, 73, 78, 102, 104, 105*

resources *45, 46, 47, 48, 49, 63, 64, 69, 72, 85, 90, 94, 101, 102, 105, 106,* 107, 114, *118, 121*

right mate *15*

s

sales *2, 9, 14, 16, 20, 50, 53, 56, 58, 59, 78, 79*

service *83, 84, 102, 107, 108*

social entrepreneurs 63, *64,* 92, 94, *118, 119*

software *51, 55*

speaking abilities *28*

start-up *107, 108, 110*

staying healthy *32*

strategic business considerations *52*

success *xii, xiii, 2, 7, 14, 17, 18, 19, 36, 39, 41, 49, 54, 55, 56, 59, 67, 68, 76, 78, 85, 90, 107, 114, 116, 123*

t

target audience *55*

tax *50, 53, 54, 57, 61, 80*

teen business *105, 121*

track and monitor your business *59*

travel *68, 108*

u

v

venture capitalist *51*

vision *xiii, 3, 16, 34, 48, 49, 50, 52, 54, 67, 71, 94, 101, 124*

visionaries *24*

volunteerism *vii, 85*

w

website *56, 105, 121*

wisdom *xi, 68, 84, 90, 91*

x

y

z

APPENDICES

CWJPPublishers offers the following references strictly for information purposes.

We do not attempt to endorse the content, online providers, or authors of these materials.

Appendix 1
Do You Really Want to Join the Entrepreneur Club?

Before making the decision to become an entrepreneur, ask yourself the following questions. Be sure to share your answers with your mate, family, and other respected business associates.

1. Why do you want to become an entrepreneur?
2. How would your family and friends react and be effected by you becoming and entrepreneur?
3. How do think your life will be like on a day-to-day basis?
4. What would you have to give up (if anything) to become entrepreneur?
5. Do you have a sense of passion for something (i.e., fashion, cars, sports, helping the homeless, feeding the hungry, creating jobs, technology, electronics, etc.)?
6. Do you have a vision? How big is your vision?
7. As a youngster, what did you always want to become when you grew up?
8. What resources do you have?
9. Do you have any existing or potential customers for your business? How can you satisfy a need that is not met?

Appendix 2
Business and Industry Resources for Entrepreneurs

This reference list is by no means complete. Be sure to do a keyword search for entrepreneurs, entrepreneurship, youth entrepreneurs, franchise(s) or franchising, start-up a business, etc. to locate additional references which may be found online, at your local bookstore, and public libraries, or business libraries on academic campuses.

Here are a few unique resources you might find helpful in researching information on entrepreneurship, business, and industry segments?

High Beam Research:
http://www.highbeam.com

Named the "**Best Online Reference Service**" by the CODiE Awards, HighBeam is a **premiere online library** where you can find research, facts, and articles. The **fee based service** offers access to **millions of articles** from newspapers like The Washington Post and The Boston Globe, magazines like The Economist and Newsweek, and journals like JOPERD and Journal of Research in Childhood Education, all in a single research Web site.

HighBeam also provides an in-depth **online library of reference works**. Research online dictionaries, including Webster's New World Dictionary and The Oxford American College Dictionary as well as encyclopedias from Britannica and Columbia.

New articles are added to HighBeam daily. Plus they have an extensive **article archive** that includes newspapers, journals, and magazine back issues dating back more than 20 years!

More than 60 million articles (new and archived)–all in one online library, including newspaper, magazine, and journal articles, book reviews, medical journals, and more!

PBS Small Business School:
http://search.smallbusinessschool.org

Small Business School is a weekly, half-hour television show that began in 1994 and has been airing ever since. The show began airing on PBS-member stations in the United States. By 1995, it was airing on IBB Voice of America TV (VOA) around the world, and cable stations throughout Canada, Latin America, South America, Africa, the Middle East, New Zealand, Poland, China and more. The Small Business School is a website where main ideas of each show episode are presented via an executive summary, transcript, case study guide and streaming video. During the initial years of production, PBS supplied had a special feed to every college and university in the USA, with case study guides provided. There are now over 2000 key points with video, transcript, and analysis from more than 200 episodes of the show that have aired on PBS stations throughout the USA. Some of the case studies have been included many of today's most business textbooks by Prentice Hall and Thomson Learning. Today, these key ideas make up the small business video section for the New York Times. **Member registration required.**

Franchise Business Review:
www.franchisebusinessreview.com

Franchise Business Review is a leading market research company in the franchise industry, assisting prospective franchise buyers through the examination process of today's leading franchise systems. Their independent franchisee satisfaction reports measure the health of any franchise system, based exclusively on the feedback of today's franchise owners... the real franchise experts!

Franchise Business Review is designed to get prospective franchise buyers the feedback they need to make a timely investment decision. The service is not intended to replace the franchise investigation process that all investors must go through. It is intended to help expedite that process and allow investors to get immediate feedback from existing franchisees.

2009 Fastest-Growing Franchises Rankings by Entrepreneur.com:
www.entrepreneur.com/franchises/rankings/fastestgrowing-115162/2009.html

Franchise Zone- Entrepreneur.com:
www.entrepreneur.com/franchises/index.html

The International Franchise Association:
www.franchise.org

The International Franchise Association, founded in 1960, is a membership organization of franchisors, franchisees, and suppliers. The Web site is dedicated to providing members and guests with a one-stop shopping experience for franchise information.

Franchise Solutions: www.franchisesolutions.com

This Web site was developed as a source of information for finding the right franchise for you. The site includes a Franchise Directory, top 10-franchise list, business opportunities, and a research franchise link.

Franchise Solutions for Women www.womensfranchises.com

Franchise Solutions for Women helps you find the right franchise business to own and take control of your career and life. Through a unique mix of business buying information, real stories about successful women franchise owners, and helpful resources and tools, you can start searching for the right business opportunity for you. Now is a great time to start exploring the wide variety of franchises and business opportunities for sale!

Military and Veteran Franchises: www.veteranfranchises.com

This Web site was developed to enable franchise ownership by veterans. It is a resource to help veterans start their own business or buy their own franchise.

U.S. Small Business: Teen Business Link Start It—Grow It—Own It www.sba.gov/teens/

Young people of today are the entrepreneurs of the future. SBA has developed a teen Website () designed to introduce young entrepreneurs to the concept of small business ownership as a viable career choice. The innovative Website helps young people shape and implement their dreams of entrepreneurship. This site features the fundamentals of starting a small business from brainstorming to evaluating the feasibility of your idea, developing the all-important business plan, learning from successful young entrepreneurs, making sound financial decisions and utilizing various entrepreneurial development services – SCORE, Junior Achievement, DECA (Distributive Education Clubs of America) and the National Academy Foundation. These valuable resources provide face-to-face counseling and training as well as online counseling and training in starting and growing a business.

ODEP - Entrepreneurship Education:
www.dol.gov/odep/pubs/fact/entrepreneurship.htm

This government site promotes encouraging future innovation through youth entrepreneurship education.

Appendix 3:
Business and Marketing Planning Resources and Tools for Entrepreneurs

This reference list is by no means complete. Be sure to do a keyword search for entrepreneurs, entrepreneurship, youth entrepreneurs, franchise(s) or franchising, start-up a business, etc. to locate additional references which may be found online, at your local bookstore, and public libraries, or business libraries on academic campuses.

Online Resource: www.SmallBizBooks.com

Entrepreneur Magazine's Business Start-Up Guides:

These guides offer clear roadmaps to success. Each guide is researched by the authors and experts of Entrepreneur Magazine. Many of the products and services are available by state.

Sample of Industry Startup Guides:

Automotive Businesses: Automobile Detailing Business, Car Wash Business; **Business Services**: Consulting Service, Executive Recruiting Service, Freelance Writing Business, Freight Brokerage Business, Grant Writing, Graphic Design Business, Import / Export Business, Information Consultant Information Marketing Business, Medical Claims Billing Service, Seminar Production Business, Staffing Service Virtual Assistant, Wholesale Distribution Business; **Food Businesses**: Bar / Club, Restaurant and Five Other Food Businesses; **Maintenance Services**: Cleaning Service, Home Inspection Service, Lawn Care / Landscaping; **Online Businesses:** *e*Bay Business, Net Services Online Business; **Personal Services**: Child-

Care Service, Coaching Business, College Planning Consultant, Event Planning Service, Gift Basket Service, Home Design Services, Kid-Focused Businesses, Personal Concierge / Shopper, Personal Training Business, Pet Businesses, Senior Care Services, Travel Services, Wedding Consultant; and **Retail Businesses**: Bed & Breakfast, Coin-Op Laundry, Crafts Business, Fashion Accessories, Floral Businesses, Hair Salon & Day Spa, Mail Order Business, Retail Store, Vending Business.

Entrepreneur Magazine's
Part time Business Start-Up Guides

If you want to start a business venture while maintaining your current employment, there are some helpful guides to starting-up part time businesses, such as: **Automobile Detailing Business, Cleaning Service, Coin-Op Laundry, Consulting Service, Crafts Business, Event Planning Service, Gift Basket Service, and Information Consultant**

Entrepreneur Magazine's
State-Specific Start-up Guides

Guides on starting a business in your state. The guides include such critical information for successful start-ups as: Valuable state-specific sample forms and letters on CD-ROM; mailing addresses, telephone numbers and websites for the federal, state, local and private agencies that will help get your business up and running; State population statistics, income and consumption rates, major industry trends and overall business incentives to give you a better picture of doing business in your State; checklists, sample forms and a complete sample business plan to assist you with numerous startup details; State-specific information on issues like choosing a legal form, selecting a business name, obtaining licenses and permits, registering to pay taxes and knowing your employer responsibilities; and Federal and state options for financing your new venture.

Entrepreneur Magazine's Startup Essentials Series

There are five comprehensive guides to help you start, finance, and market your businesses! **The series include:**

Starting Your Own Business. Filled with expert advice, this plain-English guide walks you through every aspect of starting a business.

Creating a Successful Business Plan. The easy-to-follow guide takes you step-by-step through the process of writing a plan that will win financing for your business, plus get it off to a secure start.

Financing Your Small Business. This guide reveals more than 101 sources of capital, including a state-by-state index of small-business-friendly banks.

Marketing Your Small Business. Loaded with practical, proven marketing advice and tactics, this indispensible guide can help you transform your business into a moneymaking machine.

Selling Your Products. This easy-to-follow guide takes you through all the steps you need to know to turn your products and ideas into moneymaking realities.

These guides are sold separately, or as a complete set.

Recommended Reading from Collegiate Entrepreneurs' Organization (www.uhceo.com)

Books/Magazines

Recommended Reading for Small Business (Light Reading - *Before you start your Business)*

1. *The E Myth Revisited*, 2nd edition. Michael E. Gerber, Harper Business, 2001
2. *Rich Dad Poor Dad*, Robert T. Kiyosaki, Warner Books, Inc. May 2000
3. *The Cash Flow Quadrant*, Robert T. Kiyosaki, Warner Books, Inc. May 2000

Business Planning & Start-Ups

4. *Creating A Successful Business Plan*, Entrepreneur Magazine
5. *Microsoft Small Business Kit*, Joanna L. Kotz, Microsoft Press, 2005
6. *NxLevel Guide for Entrepreneurs*, David P. Wold, NxLevel Education Foundation, Reprint July 2004
7. *Running a 21st Century Small Business*, Randy W. Kirk, Warner Business Books, 1993 & 2006
8. *Start-Up Basics*, Rieva Lesonsky, Entrepreneur Media, Inc., 1998 Edition
9. *The Successful Business Plan*, Rhonda M. Abrams, The Oasis Press / PSI Research, 1991

Improving Your Business

10. *Built to Last*, James C. Collins, Harper Business Essentials, 2002

11. *Finance & Accounting for Nonfinancial Managers*, Steven A. Finkler, Prentice Hall, 1992

12. *HyperGrow Your Business*, Curtis Clinkinbeard, Strive Publishing, 2005

13. *Market Ownership*, William A. Sherden, American Management Association, 1994

14. *Product Leadership*, Robert G. Cooper, 1999

15. *Successful Sales And Marketing*, Entrepreneur Magazine, 1999

16. *Up Against The Wal-Marts. Second Edition*, Don Taylor, AMACOM, 2005

Business Structure & Incorporating Your Business

17. *Own Your Own Corporation*, Garrett Sutton, Warner Books, Inc., 2001

18. *Incorporating your Business*, 2nd edition, Anthony Mancuso, Nolo Press, January "2004

19. *How to Form a Nonprofit Corporation*, 5th edition, Anthony Mancuso, Nolo Press, March 2002

20. Organization, Management & Networking

21. *Trump. The Art of the Deal*, Donald J. Trump with Tony Schwartz, 1987

Consulting

22. *How To Become a Consultant*, Entrepreneur Magazine, 2001

23. Howard Sherson, Anything by author

24. *Million Dollar Consulting*, Alan Weiss, McGraw-Hill, Inc., 2003

Marketing

25. *12 Simple Steps To A Winning Marketing Plan*, Geraldine A. Larkin, 1992

26. *Marketing for Growth and Profits*, Southern California Edison, 1996

27. *Marketing Your Services*, Anthony Putman

28. *Target Marketing:*, 3rd edition, Linda Pinson & Jerry Jinnett, Upstart Publishing Company 1996

Leadership

29. *Pathways To Success*, Dale Carnegie, Simon & Schuster, 1984.

30. *How To Win Friends & Influence People*, Dale Carnegie, Simon & Schuster, 1944-1984

31. *How To Stop Worrying; and Start Living*, Dale Carnegie, Simon & Schuster, 1936-1981

Management

32. *The 7 Habits of Highly Effective People*, Stephen R. Covey, Simon & Schuster, Inc. 1989

33. *Principle-Centered Leadership*, Stephen R. Covey, Simon

& Schuster, Inc. 1990

34. *First Things First*, Stephen R. Covey, Simon & Schuster, Inc. 1994

Personal Improvement

35. *Awaken The Giant Within*, Anthony Robbins, Simon & Schuster, Inc., 1992

36. *Unlimited Power*, Anthony Robbins, Ballantine Books, 1986

Wealth Accumulation

37. *The Wealthy Barber*, David Chilton, 1998 3rd Edition

38. *The Richest Man in Babylon*, George Clason, 1926

39. *The Millionaire Next Door*, Thomas J. Stanley, 1996

Amazon.com

Innovation and Entrepreneurship, Peter F. Drucker, 2006

Peter Drucker's classic book on innovation and entrepreneurship is the first book to present innovation and entrepreneurship as a purposeful and systematic discipline that explains and analyzes the challenges and opportunities of America's new entrepreneurial economy. Superbly practical, *Innovation and Entrepreneurship* explains what established businesses, public service institutions, and new ventures need to know and do to succeed in today's economy.

Although Drucker passed away in 2005, he was considered the most influential management thinker ever. The author of more than twenty-five books, his ideas have had an enormous impact on shaping the modern corporation.

Additional Online Resources:

The Vistage Company – (www.vistage.com) features an online Vistage Small Business Program, promoted as "the world's most powerful small business resource," that offers these benefits:

...a vital perspective leaders need to make the right moves to compete today and outperform tomorrow...provides the most effective sounding board for the leaders toughest decisions—fellow chief executives who have met and overcome the same challenges. This powerful forum, coupled with the best small business information available, is like getting the "trial" without the "error," and it helps Vistage members make better decisions when the stakes are highest...is a catalyst for small business ideas – it inspires our members' best thinking, challenges their assumptions and provides a platform to implement insights with confidence and precision... helps members spend less time putting out fires and more time building (focusing) for the future—the real work of the chief executive. Members gain increased clarity of purpose for their small business planning, and the peace of mind of knowing the company is positioned for continued success...the Vistage Small Business Program is about improving our members' performance so their companies can perform better. It's about continuous, accelerated, practical learning—more lasting than any one-time workshop, more actionable than any flavor-of-the-day business book—and about turning good intentions into great results.

Members are invited to join a group after a careful interview process, based on company size, competitor/vendor relationships and your specific wants and needs, to ensure they are placed in the appropriate group. Only the most qualified and dedicated candidates are selected for membership." (Vistage International, Inc. n.d.)

Entrepreneur.com
www.entrepreneur.com/

An online resource for entrepreneurs, including access and subscription to the Entrepreneur Magazine.

Entrepreneur Connect (beta)
http://econnect.entrepreneur.com

Entrepreneur Connect is a free social network where small-business owners can create a profile, explore the community, share ideas, and make connections. This site is not intended for mass self-promotion, but rather should be a positive destination where entrepreneurs can exchange real advice and make lasting connections.

Business.com
www.business.com

Business.com is the leading business search engine and directory and pay-per-click advertising network serving more than 40 million unique business users and thousands of advertisers every month. Business.com helps business decision makers quickly find what they need to manage and grow their businesses, and enables advertisers to reach these users wherever they are across the business Internet through premier partners, including Forbes, Hoovers, Financial Times and Internet.com.

Hoover's, Inc.
www.hoovers.com

Hoover's is a D&B Company that provides comprehensive insight and analysis about the companies, industries, and people that drive the economy, along with the powerful tools to find and connect to the right people to get business done.

Appendix 4: Networking Organizations and Associations for Entrepreneurs

This list is by no means inclusive of every networking organization available to entrepreneurs. Be sure to also look for local organizations where you operate.

Entrepreneurs' Organization: www.eonetwork.org

The Entrepreneurs' Organization (EO) - for entrepreneurs only - is a dynamic, global network of more than 7,000 business owners in 38 countries. Founded in 1987 by a group of young entrepreneurs, EO is the catalyst that enables entrepreneurs to learn and grow from each other, leading to greater business success and an enriched personal life.

Collegiate Entrepreneurs' Organization: www.c-e-o.org

Vision: The Collegiate Entrepreneurs' Organization[SM] is the premier global entrepreneurship network, which will serve 30,000 students, through 400 chapters and affiliated student organizations at colleges and universities.

Mission: The Collegiate Entrepreneurs' Organization[SM] informs, supports, and inspires college students to be entrepreneurial and seek opportunity through enterprise creation.

The Indus Entrepreneurs (TiE): www.tie.org

TiE-The Indus Entrepreneurs - founded in Silicon Valley in 1992 by successful entrepreneurs and professionals with roots in the Indus region.

TiE is also known as Talent Ideas and Enterprise and is today spread over 53 chapters in 12 countries.

Over 12,000 Members and 1,800 plus Charter Members - includes top Entrepreneurs, VCs, Private Equity, Angels, Law Firms, Tech & Management professionals.

Appendix 5: Resources on Social Entrepreneurship

Book:

Social Responsibility by Brooks, Arthur C., Prentice Hall (Upper Saddle River, NJ, March 2008, ISBN: 978-0132330763

This book is for the entrepreneur who seeks to understand the social and not-for-profit sectors. This content "brings together the established pedagogy of entrepreneurship with cutting edge nonprofit and public management tools: Measuring social value, Earned income, Donations and government income, Entrepreneurial fundraising and marketing, and Social enterprise business plans."

Other resources retrieved from: http://en.wikipedia.org/wiki/Social_entrepreneurship

Publications/Media-

- *Uncommon Heroes: Short film series profiling social entrepreneurs*, Skoll Foundation

- *Innovations: Technology|Governance|Globalization*, MIT Press

- Social Enterprise Reporter [1] - Innovative Business Solutions for Social Entrepreneurs

- A Developed World [2] : An online social publication that is telling stories of social entrepreneurs from around the world.

- *Can the World Change? Perspectives on Social Entrepreneurship*; http://renjie.ca.

Documentary films-

- *Social Entrepreneurship*, Ashoka: Innovators for the Public
- *The New Heroes*, PBS series profiling various individuals and projects in different market sectors around the world
- *Frontline/World Social Entrepreneurs*, PBS Frontline/World online series on social entrepreneurs

Articles

- *Social Entrepreneurship*, Sally Osberg and Roger Martin, Skoll Foundation
- *Everyone a Changemaker: Social Entrepreneurship*, Bill Drayton, Ashoka Organization
- *The Importance of Social Entrepreneurship*, Jürgen Nagler, Business4Good Organization
- *Enterprising Social Innovation: the most intriguing form of social entrepreneurship*, Greg Dees and Beth Anderson, www.sereporter.com article

Organizations

- The Laurel Centre for Social Entrepreneurship
- International Network of Social Entrepreneurs

Appendix 6:
Government and Certification Resources

- Stay abreast of the creation of President Barack Obama's Agenda and policy changes that will affect the business community, urban policy, etc.: www.whitehouse.gov www.america.gov

- Find support and guidance **for registering as a small business—or disadvantage, minority, female, or veteran-owned enterprise,** and creating and marketing your business with the federal government. www.sba.gov

- Get demographic and census data for your business planning process: www.census.gov

Look up websites for your local or regional government entities, as it relates to vendor requirements to register to do business with that entity, such as:

City government website

County government websites

State government websites

- NMSDC (National Minority Supplier Development Council) www.nmsdc.org:

Providing a direct link between corporate America and minority-owned businesses is the primary objective of the National Minority Supplier Development Council, one of the country's leading business membership organizations. It was chartered in 1972 to provide increased procurement and business opportunities for minority businesses of all sizes.

The NMSDC Network includes a National Office in New York and 39 regional councils across the country. There are

3,500 corporate members throughout the network, including most of America's largest publicly owned, privately owned, and foreign-owned companies, as well as universities, hospitals and other buying institutions. The regional councils (see NMSDC for a list of regional/local affiliates) certify and match more than 15,000 minority owned businesses (Asian, Black, Hispanic, and Native American) with member corporations that want to purchase goods and services.

- **U.S. Small Business: Teen Business Link/Start It—Grow It—Own It** is designed to introduce young entrepreneurs to the concept of small business ownership as a viable career choice. The innovative Website helps young people shape and implement their dreams of entrepreneurship. This site features the fundamentals of starting a small business from brainstorming to evaluating the feasibility of your idea, developing the all-important business plan, learning from successful young entrepreneurs, making sound financial decisions and utilizing various entrepreneurial development services – SCORE, Junior Achievement, DECA (Distributive Education Clubs of America) and the National Academy Foundation. These valuable resources provide face-to-face counseling and training as well as online counseling and training in starting and growing a business.

About the Author

Creed W. Pannell, Jr. has been an entrepreneur most of his professional life. He began his entrepreneurship ventures with the formation of Pannell Sales, Inc., serving as a manufacturer's representative for a major haircare manufacturer throughout the U.S./Southeastern Markets and the Caribbean. As CEO of Positive Publications, Mr. Pannell later created the Atlanta Metro Magazine and continues to publish the Atlanta NewsLeader, the Atlanta Business Journal, and the Weddings For Us Bridal Magazine. Mr. Pannell continues to develop new branding and marketing initiatives to enhance his product and service offerings, while creating new internet applications for extending his outreach to existing and new customers via his current business web sites.

His strong faith background and love for music, led him to create Atlanta's Gospel Choice Awards (now in its 16th year). With the success of the Gospel Choice Awards, and the growing Holy Hip-hop market, Mr. Pannell created the Youth Gospel Choice Awards (now in its 3rd year).

As an extension of the Atlanta Business Journal, Mr. Pannell created the Georgia Minority Business Awards (GMBA). Now in its 13th year, the GMBA is dedicated to helping generate awareness of the positive changes and collective successes of multi-cultural business communities. The GMBA serves as a catalyst for a new generation of business owners that will, notably serve as valuable indicators for building cultural and global relationships for the future.

Mr. Pannell has always believed in the importance of seeking opportunities to provide economically feasible and viable alternatives to the African-American community as it relates to matters of health, environmental, and lifestyle. In 2007, he co-founded It's YourChoice Natural Gas to offer the AA community a cost effective alternative for natural gas.

As an innovator, as well as a media industry entrepreneur, Mr. Pannell is always attentive to new trends in the marketplace as it relates to the marketing of his products and other services via advances in internet and communications technology. His latest business venture includes the establishment of Business Development Initiative, Inc. (BDI), a non-profit organization dedicated to encouraging youth to reach their maximum potential. Our goal is to include multiple pathways to success by providing academic and business opportunities through programs focusing on academic improvement, entrepreneurship development, community involvement, and the physical and emotional well-being of our youth.

Mr. Pannell has always believed in the youth of our communities, and is excited by the leadership, hope and vision for our country held by the first African-American to be elected president—President Barack H. Obama. He is passionate about the opportunities that will become available to enable all of us to play a vital role in the economic recovery of our country, and the strengthening of our communities.

Educated at Howard University in Washington, D.C. and the Charles Price School of Journalism in Philadelphia, PA., he is an avid golfer, and enjoys walking, swimming, reading, and traveling with his family.

Creed and his wife, Rochelle, have four children, three grandchildren, and two great-grandchildren. They reside in Atlanta, Georgia.

Notes

Notes

Notes